Routledge Education Books

Advisory editor: John Eggleston
Professor of Education
University of Keele

Keeping track of teaching

Assessment in the modern classroom

Harry Black and Patricia Broadfoot

Routledge & Kegan Paul

London, Boston, Melbourne and Henley

First published in 1982
by Routledge & Kegan Paul Ltd
39 Store Street, London WC1E 7DD,
9 Park Street, Boston, Mass. 02108, USA,
296 Beaconsfield Parade, Middle Park,
Melbourne 3206, Australia and
Broadway House, Newtown Road,
Henley-on-Thames, Oxon RG9 1EN
Set in Press Roman 10/11pt by
Columns, Reading
and printed in Great Britain by
Redwood Burn Ltd, Trowbridge, Wiltshire
© Harry Black and Patricia Broadfoot 1982
No part of this book may be reproduced in
any form without permission from the
publisher, except for the quotation of brief
passages in criticism

Library of Congress Cataloging in Publication Data

Black, Harry.

Keeping track of teaching.
(Routledge education books)
Includes bibliographical references.
1. Educational tests and measurements.
I Broadfoot, Patricia. II. Title. III. Series.
LB3051.B49   371.2'6   82-3759

ISBN 0-7100-9017-X   AACR2

Contents

Contents

Acknowledgments

This book is based to a large extent on accounts of the assessment activities in case study schools. Our first and most important acknowledgment therefore is to the teachers in these schools who both co-operated with us and allowed us to use their materials as examples of practice.

Ideas and inspiration do not develop if they are never discussed with others. Although this book is our own, most of the ideas in it are founded in the work we have carried out over the years with our colleagues. For that which is worthwhile in this book therefore we acknowledge the help of our colleagues, and in particular that of Bryan Dockrell. The errors and omissions are of course our own. To John Eggleston, our editor who has provided encouragement and advice throughout; to the editorial staff of Routledge & Kegan Paul who have been helpful and efficient in the preparation of the book; to the secretaries who accepted our many drafts with tolerance, and to Mrs Pamela Robson in particular, we owe sincere thanks.

Permission to reproduce figures and tables has kindly been given as follows: Figure 1.2, Scottish Education Department; Figure 3.2, from *Human Characteristics and School Learning* by B.J. Bloom. Copyright © 1976 McGraw-Hill Book Company. Used with the permission of the Mc-Graw-Hill Book Company; Figures 3.3, 3.4, Table 3.1, draft material from 'Tour de France', Scottish Central Committee in Modern Languages (published version Heinemann Educational Books Ltd); Figures 3.5, 3.6, 6.4, 6.5, 6.6, Table 4.2, Scottish Council for Research in Education; Figures 3.7, 4.1, Table 4.1, Western Hailes Education Centre; Figure 3.9, Bosworth College; Figure 5.1, Whitehill Secondary School; Figure 5.2, The Sutton Centre; Figure 5.3, Craigroyston School; Table 5.1 Solihull Education Authority; Figures 6.1, 6.2, 6.3, Evesham High School.

Acknowledgments

Parts of chapter 7 are based on 'A School Assessment Problem', in R. W. Fairbrother (ed.), *Assessment and the Curriculum*, Chelsea College, 1980.

Introduction

Here it is — ostensibly yet another book on assessment. Granted that in this time of contracting opportunity parents, pupils and teachers alike are increasingly concerned with the formal hurdles of the educational system, do we *really* need another book to tell us all about the nuts and bolts of the process? The answer to this question is no, and this is not what this book is about. Rather it is aimed directly at teachers, not in their capacity as examiners, which they so frequently find at best a chore, but as teachers in the classroom carrying out those activities which they regard as the most central and rewarding aspects of their job. This is a book then that is about assessment *as part of teaching*; a book which sets out to help teachers develop and use assessment procedures which are an integral and essential part of the teaching and learning process. This statement may have brought a wry smile to the faces of many readers. For many, the days of such niceties are as long gone as the enthusiasms of the 1960s and early 1970s. At a time when staffing provision and other resources are being cut to the bone, popular wisdom declares that development of any kind — in organisation, in curriculum, in assessment — is a thing of the past. This is certainly true of those approaches to development which require an elaborate super-structure of outside support and additional funding. It is not true of those new ideas which can help to enhance the quality of teaching even when falling resources and morale make a bleak climate for innovation. These are the ideas that can help the individual teacher to come that bit nearer to fulfilling his or her aims for particular children without requiring endless hours of extra curricular time and energy.

This book is particularly aimed at teachers in the 'modern' class-room. These are the classrooms in which new approaches to organisa-tion such as mixed ability and vertical grouping and the integrated day; new pupil needs such as may be found in multi-ethnic communities;

new educational objectives such as in community schools and closer links with industry, are facing teachers with the need to develop different, and above all, increasingly individualised strategies. If pedagogy and curriculum are to be tailored adequately to meet the changing classroom situations of the 1980s and beyond, traditional assessment practices must be complemented by the development and use of techniques which enable teachers to identify individual progress, diagnose problems and tailor their teaching accordingly. In recent years there has been a large number of initiatives in this area both by specialist development agencies and by classroom teachers. In this book we have tried to bring together many of the more useful of these initiatives, while setting out in more general terms the scope for a hitherto much neglected approach to assessment in which teaching concerns are paramount. The principal aim is not selection nor is it quality control. It is not motivation on the traditional carrot and stick principle. The assessment with which this book is concerned is that which will enable those teachers currently concerned with 'keeping track of teaching' to do it better.

The remit is therefore wide. It covers all the various age levels of schooling and all the various assessment tasks which present themselves to teachers from the minute-by-minute decisions underpinning classroom teaching through all manner of school recording and reporting requirements to include, finally, that information which goes from the school as a testimony to both individual attainment and instructional accountability. The book is concerned with both cognitive and non-cognitive assessment; with assessment in the whole range of school activities; with the potential for pupils as well as teachers to play their part. The approach throughout is in terms of the specific problems of a real school or department and the ways in which teachers have gone about tackling these problems. Many are the products of fundamental contradictions in the purpose of schooling itself and thus cannot be readily solved. Certainly we can offer no panaceas. All we offer is a new perspective and a new approach for some old and some new problems.

Chapter 1

The assessment scene

For want of a nail the shoe was lost
For want of a shoe the horse was lost
For want of a horse the rider was lost
For want of a rider the battle was lost
For want of a battle the kingdom was lost
And all for the want of a horseshoe nail.

If the broad domains of school subjects are kingdoms, it must be a great cause for concern amongst teachers that so many of our pupils lose them. Yet the whole assessment scene, certainly in secondary schools, is designed through certification and its parallels further down the system to report on battles and the states of kingdoms. This book is largely about the assessment of the educational equivalent of nails, and the impact that starting with the immediate needs of pupils might have on assessment and reporting throughout the school. Each school and each class is different and, hence, the precise solution to assessment problems will not be the same for any two teachers or schools. Yet the same issues and problems tend to crop up in every school: the same dilemmas and the same tensions. Thus, although each chapter starts with the experience of a particular school, we believe our discussion of these idiosyncratic initiatives will be recognisable to the majority of our readers. Perhaps most familiar will be the caricature of traditional practice which sets the scene for the problems discussed in this book.

Where all men have been before

Old Normgrade Grammar School, unlike most of the other schools described in this book does not exist. Despite that you may recognise it better than the others. In fact you might have been there. Or do you work there?

At Old Normgrade assessment is looked upon as being very important. Regular continuous assessment tests are given by every teacher and interspersed with equally regular examinations. Reports on academic achievement are sent regularly to parents, who, if their representatives on the parents/teachers associations are anything to go by, wait with

1

anticipation to discover how well their children have done compared with the others in their class. Nor has the school spurned the march of progress, at least as it sees it. Letter grades (A to E) are given instead of percentages in the lower school, and considerable use is made of the local computer centre's mark-standardisation procedures, even for the first-year grades.

Let us look more closely at what this assessment system means to teachers, pupils and parents. What sort of return do they get for the substantial effort put into creating and marking tests and examinations and writing reports?

The setting and the planning of continuous assessment has been left to each department and their solutions vary considerably. As an example, however, we will look at the history department. The department has developed its course on a modular basis of work, and has set out clearly defined aims and objectives for each unit of work, including some interesting ideas from a humanities project on which one of the younger members of staff worked at one time. These include, amongst a series of concepts which run longitudinally through the whole history course, objectives such as 'the development of initiative' and 'the ability to distinguish objectively a variety of points of view on a historical situation'. Perhaps most interesting of all is that the department has distinguished a core of work which they expect all pupils to attain, as well as a series of extensions for those who attain the core quickly. In short, the history department is progressive, thoughtful and diligent.

The head of the department, Mrs Longright, has had experience as a CSE moderator and now sets and marks for one of the examination boards. Not only has she heard of item discrimination in tests, she knows what it means (a correlation of those correct in both item and test) and has been on several examination board courses on item writing. With such a background, she has set out to apply her developed ideas on assessment to a new curriculum. But that it is where we begin to find contradictions.

To begin with, the main *raison d'être* of the enterprise is to accumulate information for her continuous assessment markbooks. These marks will contribute to an attainment grading in history for report cards. But the school policy is that these reports should be in a 'normal' distribution, i.e., 10 per cent A; 20 per cent B; 40 per cent C; 20 per cent D; 10 per cent E which means that Mrs Longright's tests must spread her pupil marks in as close an approximation to this as possible. Now through her examination board experience she knows how to do this by choosing items for her tests which discriminate between 'more able' and 'less able' pupils. To the unsuspecting, of course, this may look like a fortunate coincidence for the department, but one of her colleagues does not think so. 'Why,' he inquires, 'if I succeed in teaching our agreed intentions to 70 per cent of my class, do I have to tell half of them that they have failed?' The only answer that could be mustered had 'school assessment policy' as its central argument.

And then there is the problem of the tests themselves. To keep marking time to a minimum (a strategy heartily endorsed by the whole department, who want to use their non-teaching time to create new worksheets), most of the tests were multiple choice items which had been adopted or adapted from published collections of questions or past external examination questions. Now previous research has shown that about 70 per cent of such items test knowledge of facts and specifics. However, the aims and objectives of the course, which have been agreed upon by the whole department, include a strong emphasis on concept attainment, development of historical skills of inquiry and more open-ended intentions, such as the encouragement of initiative. And it was becoming clear to the department, looking at its testing procedure, that these latter objectives were not being taken into account. There seemed to be an imminent danger that despite their admirable curriculum planning, the limitations of their testing procedure would result in a situation similar to that described by Wilhelms: 'If a History teacher says he is aiming for big generalisations but organises his evaluative feed-back in terms of the memorisation of facts, his students will soon attend to the facts — and so eventually will he.'[1]

However, the reason for looking at Old Normgrade is not so much to criticise it as to describe it, because its problems and its practices are familiar, and indeed it is those that give rise to our writing this book.

How, for example, are the report card grades decided? Quite progressively, the head has decided that the grade should not simply comprise a single mark from the end of term examinations. Continuous assessment, including a 10 per cent 'effort' component, is to account for 40 per cent of the grade. The remaining 60 per cent is to come from an end of term examination with 10 per cent of this coming from a 'use of language' mark, an innovation resulting from the head's recent participation in a conference on Language Across the Curriculum. Quite how this mark distribution was arrived at, nobody is quite sure, nor is anyone sure how the parents of a third-year pupil are to decide whether 57 per cent in physics means that he is a lazy genius with a spidery scrawl, or a hard-working neat writer with severe problems in the subject.

Although generally a fairly content establishment, especially amongst the more senior staff, it is perhaps a reflection of the importance now attached to assessment that the greatest row in recent years broke out over second-year reporting which was the basis for subject choice in

3

certificate courses in the third year. Asterix, the head of modern languages, had, in front of the whole staff, accused Crotchett, the Latin man, of cheating. The charge was that in order to encourage pupils to take Latin at the expense of a second modern language, he was lowering his standards to such an extent that anyone could pass. Not only was he creaming off the best scholars by giving them the impression that they were far better at Latin than French, but he was also misleading many 'average' pupils who would be better employed in other subjects. Crotchett was unmoved and made it clear that he felt that most of his students were getting high marks because they had learned everything he had intended they should learn. Now everyone knew what Crotchett was up to and that Asterix was quite correct in his accusation. Crotchett had never really worked out what his intentions were other than to keep a healthy number in Latin where the failure rate was very high. What was to be done?

By coincidence, the head had a visit from a young statistician from the local college computing department. The school had never really been successful in persuading the departments to impose a rigid normal distribution on their marks. But apparently the college had a mark-standardisation programme which would produce a normal distribution of grades for each department from the teachers' raw marks. Crotchett's marks would now be comparable with those of Asterix and there would be no more nasty scenes in the staffroom. The nagging doubt did not seem to linger in many minds that perhaps Crotchett was right in saying that a large proportion of his class had attained what he intended, even if his aims were set too low.

And what of the reports going out to parents? It is now some years since the school gave up the idea of giving rank orders for individual pupils in each class as it was felt that the standardised grades were giving comparative information without making it obvious that many of the pupils were consistently poor in comparison with their peers. So now the report simply states the general attainment grades for each subject with a space for comments from each teacher.

How does this relate to teaching? We have seen that the history department carefully sets out a variety of intentions for each unit at 'core' and 'extension' levels. Interesting and highly successful teaching techniques are giving good results in the classroom. But what the department now needs are assessment techniques which will give pupil, teacher and parent feedback on the whole range of learning intentions, and point out areas of individual strength and weakness. Instead, they end up with a single general attainment score related, by and large, to those intentions which were easy to assess. These scores are then statistically adjusted into grades which give little insight into the real attainment of student and teacher. Nevertheless, now that most of the more glaring shortcomings of their assessment procedures have been removed, most of the staff at Old Normgrade are reasonably confident that they have incorporated the best of the new without sacrificing the lessons of experience enshrined in the more traditional assessment practices. Indeed, assessment rarely figures in their conversation. By far the most important concern is the development of subject expertise and keeping up to date with new teaching methods. Equally, parents are happy with the familiar style of the reports they receive. They trust the fairly traditional approach of the school to continue to give primacy to the supremely important goal of public examination success for which the school has long been noted.

We have invented Old Normgrade as an illustration of the contemporary assessment situation in many schools. At Old Normgrade, as elsewhere, individual teachers and departments are pursuing new curriculum and assessment practices as new needs manifest themselves in the educational process. This has tended to result in contradiction between the old and the new, between teaching and assessment concerns. Consequently the changes that have taken place have been slow and difficult. The other schools we will write about are real. They are all moving away from the Old Normgrade model in a number of ways and are probably a lot less typical than our fictional school. All are in a state of change and are not so much models of practice as case studies of interesting developments, where schools and individual teachers are searching for ways of minimising the contradictions between teaching and assessment by making assessment an integral part of curriculum and, hence, classroom learning.

Assessment in perspective

Old Normgrade is something of a caricature. Its problems and tensions will nevertheless be familiar to many teachers. The problems which we have highlighted include the difficulty of pursuing inter-subject comparability by means of mark-standardisation despite the fact that progress may really be greater in one department than another; the difficulty of not discouraging pupils by rating them against each other, rather than against their own previous performance, in order not to raise false hopes; the difficulty of designing assessment procedures which reinforce the whole range of teaching objectives and not least the difficulty of finding time to even begin to think about assessment, let alone to design and operate potentially more time-consuming techniques. These are just some of the more common problems.

At a more general level, the tensions will be familiar to many teachers. To pick them all out would require half a chapter, but, in particular, we must note: the dominance of external certification versus the *learning* needs of individual pupils; engrained teacher attitudes versus a willingness to consider useful innovations; the needs of pupils who have already attained the teachers' basic intentions versus the needs of those who require more time and help; the demands exercised by reporting versus the potential of assessment designed to help pupils to learn; the tendency for the limitations of assessment procedures to undervalue many of the more fundamental teaching intentions; and, the appeal of the apparent objectivity of numbers as it militates against curriculum intentions that cannot be measured quantitatively.

At the same time, it is unlikely that most teachers will have given such problems more than scant attention, partly because they prefer to spend their all-too-limited free time on tasks they consider to be more directly concerned with fostering learning, and partly because assessment is generally considered to be a pretty boring subject anyway. Tests and examinations, records and reports, come round with monotonous regularity, a necessary chore, but one which all too often interferes with the main business of teaching. Curriculum, on the other hand, is a matter which claims much more attention and interest. The departmental structure within the school and the ladders of promotion within the whole system as well as most teachers' strong subject interest result in a massive effort in the creation of idiosyncratic worksheets and teaching syllabuses. Publications, in-service courses, advisory services, curriculum development groups and the mammoth output of the educational publisher have all conspired to make curriculum development into a major growth industry.

In contrast, assessment, which to most people means the same thing as rank orders, percentages, pass/fail and certificates, has been left far behind in the popular development stakes. With the exception of the active involvement of some secondary school teachers in marking, moderating and setting for the examination boards, very few teachers are aware of the considerable variety of uses for assessment and the many approaches which have been developed to improve the quality and value of the process.

We hope that this book will show that the full potential of assessment in helping teachers and pupils has seldom been realised in the past. It could well be argued that the need for a more divergent look at school and class assessment policies was not as obvious when the great majority of children sat in neat rows of desks in traditional classrooms; when the primary school curriculum and assessment policy was dominated by

11-plus; when external certificates were designed solely with the 'more able' secondary school pupils in mind.

Today, however, almost every classroom has been affected by some change which means more than a fresh look at *what* we teach. The whole fabric of teaching and learning has been rewoven by the introduction of the integrated day, open plan classrooms, mixed ability classes, pupils who are forced to stay at school until they are sixteen when many of them feel that they would rather be elsewhere, language and cultural considerations amongst ethnic minorities, movements towards individualised learning, middle schools, sixth-form colleges, team teaching and integrated studies, to mention but a few. At the same time, most primary schools have seen the end of the 11-plus, which has left a vacuum for many in focusing their assessment policies, while in contrast secondary schools have been forced further into the stereotype of the external examination-dominated curriculum and assessment policy by the introduction of the CSEs in England and Wales and the 'banding' of the Scottish 'O' Grades. The net result is that many primary school teachers are at a considerable loss to know how best to direct their assessment policies while their secondary contemporaries have a considerable struggle on their hands if they want to focus on anything other than assessment for reporting.

The purposes of assessment

To take a step back from the running tension between the practice and potential of assessment procedures, let us look briefly at the full range of uses to which assessment can be applied. Figure 1.1 shows three main reasons for assessment; for reporting, for guidance and for diagnosis.

Assessment for reporting

Few people would dispute that reporting on student attainment, both periodically while the student is still moving through the school and at the end of his school life, is an important function of schools. A recurring theme throughout this book, however, will be that while most people would find it very difficult to argue that reporting is the *reason* for education, the external assessment model, both in primary schools, where the 11-plus is still retained and, especially, in secondary schools where the curriculum is dominated by the external examination system exerts an influence on all assessment which is out of proportion

7

to even its own requirements. In other words, the external assessment model is applied in many cases where a different approach would in no way distract from the efficiency of schools in getting their students over the final hurdle and would indeed result in a *greater* degree of success amongst many students and a much richer reflection of the whole range of attainments resulting from their work in school.

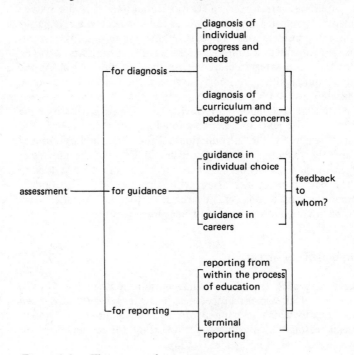

Figure 1.1   The reasons for assessment

As we will see later in the book, this alternative approach which emphasises the role of assessment as an aid to learning has resulted in a number of novel and interesting ideas on how reporting might be better suited to the requirements of the modern classroom. At this stage, however, it might be valuable to start our thinking on how attainment might be reported by tackling the vital question of *what* might be reported rather than how it will be presented.

To go back to Old Normgrade for a moment, it is clear that with the exception of a small element of the total reporting grade for 'effort', and a typically cryptic 'comment' from the teachers, the only aspect of a pupil's work in school on which 'judgment' is passed is his cognitive attainment, i.e. how much is learned about the subject matter of the disciplines in which he has worked. But is this sufficient to reflect the myriad of reasons why a student is in school? Most formal and informal statements of curriculum objectives would set out·a range of objectives of which the development of cognitive skills is only one aspect. Typical in this respect are the aims set out in the report of the Munn Committee,[2] which was set up by the Secretary of State for Scotland to examine the structure of the curriculum in the third and fourth years of the Scottish Secondary School:

(1) The development of knowledge and understanding, both of the self and of the social and physical environment.
(2) The development of *cognitive skills* including the ability to read, to handle numbers, to communicate effectively in speech and in writing, to interpret diagrammatic material, to detect fallacies in argument, to hypothesise, etc.; the development of *interpersonal skills* including, for example, the ability to get on with others, to be appropriately assertive or acquiescent, to behave appropriately in groups, in arguments and other social situations, etc.; and the development of *psychomotor* skills such as the ability to play games, to carry out experiments, to cook, to make objects, etc.
(3) To contribute to the affective development of students; to be tolerant and fair, to respect evidence and to be committed to the rational solution of problems, to be resourceful, self-reliant and hard working, to take responsibility for their own learning, etc.
(4) To reflect the demands of society; pupils must acquire knowledge and skills which relate to the world of work, to leisure, to personal relationships and family life, etc.

The report also stated that:

we reject the view that the curriculum should be exclusively concerned with cognitive attainment and that other capacities — like social competence, moral concern or skills in practical activities — should be developed in only less formal ways. . . . We consider that all of them must be provided for in the deliberately planned series of learning experiences which make up the formal curriculum.

Yet at the same time the typical Scottish end of term report contained the information shown in Figure 1.2. Is this a fair reflection of the whole range of aims set out for schools by the Munn Committee, which are surely not all that different from those pursued by most schools throughout the United Kingdom? Does it totally reflect what

SECONDARY SCHOOL REPORT/RECORD

Register Class of the pupil

Name of school

Name of pupil

Note to parents

The object of this report is to inform you of your child's attainment and progress in the subjects shown, and also to provide an estimate of whether, *in relation to his/her own age, aptitude and ability,* this progress can be regarded as satisfactory.

You are also advised in the report of the degree of interest shown by your child in each subject.

Where applicable, the set in which your child has been placed for a particular subject is indicated by an entry such as 2/3 — meaning that he/she has been placed in the second of three sets.

For attainment, pupils are assessed in relation to all the pupils in their class on a five-point scale as follows:

A *(well above average),* B *(above average),* C *(average),* D *(below average),* E *(well below average)*

If you wish more information you are welcome to call at the school.

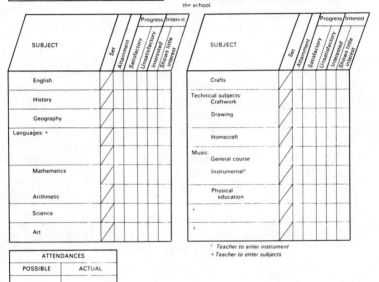

SUBJECT	Set	Attainment	Progress — Satisfactory	Progress — Unsatisfactory	Interest — Interested	Interest — Shows little interest
English						
History						
Geography						
Languages: +						
Mathematics						
Arithmetic						
Science						
Art						

SUBJECT	Set	Attainment	Progress — Satisfactory	Progress — Unsatisfactory	Interest — Interested	Interest — Shows little interest
Crafts						
Technical subjects: Craftwork						
Drawing						
Homecraft						
Music: General course						
Instrumental*						
Physical education						
+						
+						

* Teacher to enter instrument
+ Teacher to enter subjects

ATTENDANCES	
POSSIBLE	ACTUAL

Remarks (to be entered only when necessary):

_____ *(date)*   _____ *(Head Teacher)*

Figure 1.2   The typical Scottish report form in use before 1977

goes on in pupil team-work, in resource-based learning, in debate, in the basic skills? Is it a source of motivation for the young school-leaver, for the bright, active-minded pupil who can strip down a motorbike in half an hour, but has difficulty explaining Newton's Laws in writing, for the pupil who shows himself to be a natural leader in fieldwork and in sport? Or is it perhaps a relic from Old Normgrade with which most teachers feel 'safe' out of familiar habit, or perhaps they feel wary of making judgments in areas where 'standards' are more problematic and assessments harder to substantiate with apparently objective evidence?

Assessment for diagnosis

Despite what we think to be the attraction of some of the interesting alternatives to traditional reporting which we will consider, if the only impact on the reader's thinking was the possibility of altering their reporting procedures, then this book would have failed abysmally. And the reason for this is that we would have failed to answer the questions 'Why do we have assessment?', 'Who is assessment for?' and 'What use can we make of the results of assessment?' It was perfectly clear that in Old Normgrade, the teachers assessed their pupils to fill their mark-books with information which would provide the basis for reports to parents according to school policy. But despite current practice in most schools this 'school assessment is what is assessed in schools' argument will not stand up to inspection. To begin with, it would be very wrong to assume that the pattern of assessment as it is in schools today has always been the same. For example, Ingenkamp[3] tells us that,

> As long as organised learning processes have existed, the assessment of progress has been made by teachers. This is the feedback which students require in order to direct their own learning processes and achieve the greatest possible success. So long as the selection of individuals for specific roles in society was by other means (such as birth and background), learning was an accessory or embellishment to the inherited role, and not the prerequisite for a particular social status; feedback fulfilled no selective function and so remained socially irrelevant.

Of course, few people would disagree that competition by merit for high status and high reward positions is preferable to allocation by privilege. But it is becoming increasingly clear that up to now this has been achieved only at a price. Not only has a vast amount of time, money and effort had to be devoted to it, but for most people, assessment has become synonymous with judgment and certification.[4]

In contrast, the feedback which students require in order to direct their own learning processes and achieve their greatest possible success, and which in this book we see as coming from diagnostic assessment has been relegated to a function which many teachers see as optional and few treat as a high priority.

Yet, as we will see in chapter 3, diagnostic assessment and the teaching strategies which go with it have been shown by many studies to offer substantial benefits to both the student and the teacher. To draw an analogy, if a novice was having difficulty growing cauliflowers in his garden he would be little further forward if an expert horticulturist came along, assessed the stunted, caterpillar-infested end product and presented the already disheartened gardener with a rosette entitled 'failure'. For a start, he already knew that he couldn't grow cauliflowers, and the terminal assessment of the expert's judgment in no way remedied his plight. The only solution in sight is crazy paving. Suppose, however, that our friendly neighbourhood horticulturist had come along in time to point out where the novice was making his mistakes. 'Failure' would still be the first message, but as it is backed up by an immediate and helpful remedy then it is seen as a positive form of assessment and not as a criticism.

Diagnostic assessment in schools follows exactly the same model. It can give the pupil information on the areas of his work he has or has not mastered. It provides the teacher with the feedback on which to base the next appropriate learning activity. It also contributes to the evaluation of the suitability of her teaching strategy and her curriculum by pointing up areas which her whole class found difficult.

The approach is common enough in remedial education. It has been around in primary schools for many years where children are having reading problems. Furthermore, it is basically the approach followed by the 'good' teacher as she walks around the room discussing points of difficulty with individual pupils. Yet despite its clear potential, it is only recently that a start has been made to provide resources which will help teachers to apply it more systematically in the normal classroom.

Assessment for guidance

Teachers, especially in secondary schools, have always been involved in helping their pupils to make decisions. Important choices have to be made about which subjects to study, which courses to follow and which careers to pursue. In many cases, such as in the application of selective examinations, including the 11-plus, or where entry into an A level course in a given school requires previous attainment of a comparable O level, the help which a teacher can give is fairly limited. But where the pupil is making decisions about his choice of subject in secondary school, or making his choice of a career towards the end of his school life, it would seem that teacher guidance might be of considerable importance. And while the transition from school to work will only be our concern tangentially, when we look at 'terminal' reporting systems in chapter 6, the notion of how teacher assessment relates to guidance advice which might be given to pupils regarding their choice of subjects lower down the school is an implicit recurring concern of all assessment procedures.

In recent years the significance of the choice which pupils have to make on transition from the early years of secondary school to the more formal courses which may lead to a pupil being (or not being) presented for an external examination has increased dramatically, because in many cases this may be the first occasion on which he comes up against the potential trauma of 'differentiation'. In the past, and indeed where the process is still practised today, 'selective' assessment on transition from primary to secondary school considerably circum-scribed the role of the teacher. Today, however, with formal selection increasingly declining in importance, the potential for teacher involve-ment in such guidance, and for pupil reliance on this, is more crucial. The question which the teacher must ask is how she might best approach this enhanced responsibility, and how she can collect the information required.

Where guidance advice is given to pupils on subject choice, practice, and, in particular, the relationship between assessment and guidance, varies considerably. In some schools it is made clear to pupils that they will only be allowed to take certain subjects or courses if their per-formance in an examination, or over a period of continuous assessment, is satisfactory. In others decisions are formally made in consultation with guidance staff or principal subject teachers. In some a recom-mendation is included in the 'option' sheet which the pupil is given, while in a few cases, pupils are allocated to courses without being given a choice. Ryrie, Furst and Lauder[5] found that where there was a systematic procedure of providing guidance advice on subject choice, some pupils felt that they had a fairly free choice and some that the teachers took account of things like career intentions, but the overall impression of the pupils was that teachers made recommendations or decisions largely on their marks, and that choices were available only if a pupil had done well in a number of subjects. Furthermore, the researchers concluded that not only was this the impression of pupils, but also of parents.

13

Now it is likely that the majority of teachers, pupils and parents would accept this situation as given, and because of the clear importance of subject choice to pupils in secondary schools we would have included a chapter in this book to deal with assessment for subject choice. However, Ryrie *et al.* reach another interesting conclusion, which is that the advice given to pupils as a result of such assessment has little effect on subject choice. Furthermore, they go on to say that:

> By the time when option forms had to be completed, some fairly clear assumptions had come to be generally accepted by all concerned. . . . What we are suggesting is that it was these mutually accepted assumptions rather than any direct influences on the pupils which produced the patterns we have observed in the subjects studies.

In essence then, the argument seems to be that pupil choices are governed by an assumption which they make about their 'general ability', the assumption which they make about the appropriateness of certain subjects in the light of what they think about their own ability, and perhaps most important, by the message they receive *in the long term* from their teachers about their ability to cope with certain aspects of learning. If this is the case, and it seems to us to be a sound argument, the outcome of formal assessment procedures to allocate or direct pupils to subject choices is of little consequence. Furthermore, the specification of criteria for entry to certificate courses, which can be included in a single examination, or even a series of continuous assessment tests, and which will adequately predict success at the end of the course is extremely difficult. It seems to us, therefore, that the most successful developments in assessment for guidance will be in those procedures which both help the pupil to come to a better understanding of his own strengths, weaknesses and interests and allow the teacher to become better acquainted with the needs of individual pupils. Such outcomes are likely to arise from the development of teacher skills in assessment for diagnosis, which is the subject of chapter 3.

Tensions and constraints

It is one thing to be aware of the full range of uses to which assessment can be applied and the shortcomings of our present approaches in fulfilling them. But it is quite another to put potential solutions into practice. Figure 1.3 suggests a number of tensions and constraints which have to be taken into account.

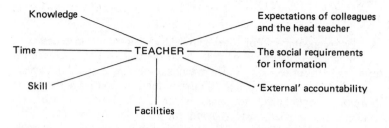

Figure 1.3   Tensions and constraints influencing teachers' assessment practices

Knowledge

One of the most basic obstacles to the uptake of assessment development is that the people who matter, and that means practising teachers and head teachers, do not have easy access to the many interesting ideas and resources which they might choose to try out if they were aware of their existence. One of the main reasons for writing this book is to help to fill that gap in teachers' knowledge. In all truth it cannot be claimed that there is an impressive track record in persuading practising teachers that it may be worth devoting some of their very limited time to reading such books. Nor for that matter is there much evidence of local authorities providing the resources to allow teachers substantial periods of in-service training to bring themselves up to date with developments in assessment.

From the point of view of the educationist working outside the classroom, there can be no doubt that dissemination of research and development findings has always been a weak link in the system. This is partly because research reports have to satisfy two audiences; the teacher, who wants clear unambiguous usable materials which she can adopt or adapt for her own classroom, and other researchers and 'academic' educationists, who perform a highly critical peer evaluation function which contributes to a high standard of work, but which, if their demands are to be satisfied, can make it difficult going for the casual reader. Furthermore, in most school subjects, or local areas, there is not a tradition of disseminating assessment (or teaching) techniques with anything approaching the enthusiasm associated with the discussion of curriculum issues at teachers' centres, or in subject association journals. What is needed is a greater awareness amongst teachers of the potential importance of assessment accompanied by a much more effective means of making examples of good practice available to them.

Skill

A clear concomitant of the 'knowledge' constraint in assessment development is the degree of skill which the teacher has developed for using the various techniques. There tends to be a mystique about assessment techniques which is largely unwarranted. Jargon plays its part in 'turning people off', not least where apparently straightforward teachers' handbooks insist in giving, for example, the formula for the point biserial correlation coefficient and the Kuder-Richardson reliability test, both of which may be important to the test-construction specialist, but which to the average teacher are of little consequence!

The first requirement for successful assessment development in schools is not that every Latin teacher becomes a statistics specialist as well, but that all teachers develop the skill to be intelligent *users* of the various techniques and instruments available from elsewhere. We saw this happening in Old Normgrade, where the head teacher decided (inadvisedly perhaps) to use the local computing centre's marks-standardisation package. Similarly, most local computing centres have item analysis packages available which can give the teacher a considerable amount of data on multiple choice items simply by providing the centre with the correct answers to the test and having the students answer the questions in whatever format the centre uses. The computerised version of the SCRE Pupil Profile[6] system which is described in detail in chapter 6 will provide a variety of arrays of pupil report from the teacher's original assessment record. In all of these cases the type of information which the teacher has to give to the data processing centre is very straightforward and not impracticable for the pupils themselves to record. The crucial question is whether the teacher has been given help to develop the skill to make the appropriate choice of techniques for any given problem.

Expectations of colleagues and the head teacher

Schools are social systems and consequently a change made by a single teacher, by the infant department, by a secondary subject department or by the head teacher will have an effect on everyone in the system and not just the individual or group which instigates the change. This is no idle sociological comment on the obvious. For example, in many schools one of the greatest obstacles facing teachers who want to introduce a programme of diagnostic assessment is the expectation of school assessment policies that the feedback from the continuous components of assessment should be presented in the form of grades in a normal distribution. However, as we have seen above, diagnostic assessment simply does not attempt to conform to the 'normal distribution' expectation. The obvious problem facing the teachers who have come to see diagnostic assessment as the best method of making continuous assessments is that they are doing something which no longer conforms with the expectations of their colleagues and the head teacher, and consequently substantial and sometimes difficult renegotiations have to take place.

In a wider perspective, this underlines the fact that school systems are essentially rather conservative. In some ways they have to be, because the children for whom they exist are not guinea pigs. At the same time, however, reluctance to change can lead to atrophy and the combination of complacency and apathy which has, for example, continued to allow the external certification model so easily to dominate the secondary school assessment scene.[7] The solution is in sound, convincing and controlled evaluation of assessment development designed specifically to cater for the needs of the modern classroom.

The social requirements for information

Not only are schools social systems in their own right, but clearly they are an important element of a wider social network which requires information about the schools' students. In addition to the regular reports provided to parents, schools have considerable demands on them for reference to prospective employers and other educational establishments, information on individuals for the social services, feedback to the students themselves for guidance decisions, and for internal decision-making purposes. On the one hand, this means that there is considerable tension influencing what information can and should be provided by the school, not least because the information contained in conventional reporting systems, such as that shown in Figure 1.2, is totally inadequate for the varied needs of the whole school population.

These tensions and constraints are likely to be particularly marked where the need for information goes beyond the straightforward reporting of subject attainment as we shall see in chapters 4 and 6. For example, one survey of teacher attitudes[8] to assessing characteristics of pupils other than academic achievement found 44 per cent of teachers in favour, 44 per cent against, and the rest unsure. This kind of ambivalence is widespread although the fact that, at least to our knowledge, all schools are willing to provide character references to prospective employers and detailed reports for higher education is a strong argument for some systematic attempt to collect such information.

17

'External accountability'

A clarion call of the late 1970s and the 1980s is 'accountability'. The exact meaning of the term when it is used in education is somewhat obscure, but its implications are clear. Schools must be willing and able to submit themselves to public scrutiny to justify what they are doing. They need to be able to show that they are succeeding in fulfilling their stated intentions and especially any requirements such as 'standards of numeracy' which the establishment sees fit to make of all schools. This latter role of assessment is particularly associated in England and Wales with the work of the Assessment of Performance Unit of the Department of Education and Science which was set up in 1974 to monitor standards in each of the major curricular areas. In chapter 5 we discuss the novel and significant demands that this movement is making on schools. Not only are schools as a whole to be responsible for the general standards attained by pupils,[9] but schools are increasingly being encouraged to engage in self-evaluation of the quality of the educational experiences they offer.[10] No school can hold itself aloof from these trends and it may well be that they will serve more than any other recent development in educational provision to promote active consideration of the new assessment approaches required for the modern classroom.

Facilities and time

Teachers are very poorly supported by services and facilities to back up their teaching. Many paper and pencil tests yield doubtful results, not because of the nature of the content, but because they are scribbled in the teacher's handwriting instead of being typed. Teachers have to perform tedious and unnecessary marking of simple multiple choice or completion tests which could quite easily be marked by a clerk. They have to work without auxiliary help in the classroom, where many of the simple managerial chores such as checking registers, giving out worksheets and textbooks, and setting up slide projectors could quite easily be done by an assistant, and so release the teacher to work with individuals. Yet while plumbers have their mates, British Rail engine drivers have their firemen, joiners have their apprentices and even (some) headmasters have their secretaries, it is increasingly unlikely that the teacher will be able to call on any other resources than her own time, her own skill and her own enthusiasm to aid her in developing new approaches to classroom assessment.

The implication of all this is that if new ideas in assessment are to work, rather than join the pile of good ideas on the (rejected) good ideas heap, then they must be tailored to fit the time and facilities which are available in schools. The problem is that 'available' time is a contentious issue. For example, a conclusion reached by a group of teachers and researchers working on a project to develop means of reliably assessing personal characteristics of pupils[11] was that a much improved and objective scaling system for the assessment of affective pupil characteristics by teacher observation could be created for a school using techniques developed on a research basis in about the same time as it takes to set out and mark an end of term examination. Thereafter the use of the observation schedule would take up a very small proportion of teacher time, but would yield considerable benefits in making teachers much more aware of the particular attributes, problems and potential of the individual students in their classes. But, as we have already suggested, the existing order of perceived priorities is weighed heavily against such assessment development. Even if we could persuade teachers that the end of term examination or the development of yet more worksheets was less important than sound and relevant classroom assessment procedures, traditional practices and expectations in the school as a whole are even slower to shift and are likely to impede such initiatives still further.

The way forward

In this chapter we have sketched in some of the tensions affecting traditional school assessment practices. We have identified some of the conflicting needs which are the source of these tensions. And we have briefly discussed some of the reasons why these problems are likely to become increasingly pressing in the future. This is the reason for this book. Our approach will be essentially an optimistic one, taking as our starting point some examples of the best practice which have been accomplished with no special resources and are thus open to emulation by any teacher sharing the same concerns. Exactly what these concerns are likely to be is the subject of the next chapter.

Chapter 2

Problems in practice

Tradition and change

The mile or so of suburban street that might separate Hilltop Primary School from Old Normgrade Grammar belies the much greater distance that separates the educational philosophy of the two schools. The formal layout of the Grammar School becomes a series of bright open 'areas' at Hilltop. Here there are no classrooms, no desks in serried rows, no bells. Children are scattered throughout the various nooks and crannies of the open plan building, some gathered round a teacher, some watching a school programme on television, some working industriously in twos and threes with little apparent supervision. Outside, other children are doing mysterious things with weather instruments or less mysterious things with the cages of the various school pets. A number of adults are working with the children in their various activities. Some are parents who come in regularly to lend a hand, others are teachers. Most move about continuously, helping a child here, exchanging a word with a colleague there. Some of the teachers, though, are more easily recognisable by the circle of eager upturned faces surrounding them as they listen to children's 'news' or tell a story.

The explanation for some of the differences between Old Normgrade Grammar and Hilltop Primary are obvious — the architecture and the age of the children in particular. But if we were to talk to the head teacher at Hilltop we would soon see that the differences between the two schools are much more profound. At Hilltop School, the head teacher believes in keeping a balance between inquiry-based learning and formal teaching. He believes in the need to encourage children to be creative, self-reliant and self-critical. He wants them to be happy and purposefully engaged, readily finding a sense of achievement in the various tasks they undertake. He sees himself as friend and colleague to

20

the other teachers and encourages a maximum of informality in every aspect of school life.

But if Old Normgrade Grammar and Hilltop Primary differ in their outward appearance and the ways in which lessons and teaching are organised, fundamentally they are not so different in what they are seeking to achieve. Both schools try to provide a balanced curriculum of practical and theoretical work, arts and sciences; both put great emphasis on English and maths; both want to encourage pupils to identify with the school and value sport in this respect. Both want to provide the maximum opportunity for each child to achieve in relation to his strengths and weaknesses.

Most of us are familiar with schools like Old Normgrade Grammar and Hilltop Primary; both are likely to be near where we live; we may teach in one or the other − our children may attend them. Equally, most of us are fairly familiar with the kinds of assessment carried out at Old Normgrade − class tests, end of term examinations, GCEs, the traditional school report: 'doesn't try hard enough, could do better . . .'. We are unlikely to be equally familiar with the ways in which the apparently haphazard activities at Hilltop are part of a carefully orchestrated programme of learning with its very different, but equally central, system of assessments and records.

In this chapter we shall describe what happens at Hilltop in some detail in order to highlight the very different role which assessment must play in the informal, individualised learning environment of the modern classroom. But if the need for new approaches and new techniques is most visible in those years of schooling − primary, junior and lower secondary − before the constraints of the external examination and the formal syllabus begin to take effect, the need is just as real, if less visible, in the formal classrooms of Old Normgrade Grammar, if teaching is genuinely to relate to the strengths and weaknesses of the individual child.

Most secondary schools have been left untouched by the far-reaching changes which have swept through junior schools in the wake of the wave of 'progressive', child-centred philosophy, greatly strengthened by the demise of the 11-plus. Thus in some ways, as the case studies of subsequent chapters will show, the secondary teacher, who wishes to integrate assessment with teaching, is yet more desperate for new techniques than her primary colleagues in order to overcome the negative and constraining effects of formal testing. Equally, the new demands that new types of classroom organisation, such as mixed ability teaching, are making on secondary school teachers also make the need for new means of 'keeping track of teaching' very pressing. How, for example, do you organise the individual or group pacing of learning without both suitable curricular materials *and* a simple way of recording who has completed what unit of work. Nor is it sufficient merely to record work done, since the teacher will want to have some overview of each individual child's general progress, his strengths and weaknesses and his interests. Not only is this kind of approach likely to be more familiar to the teacher in the more informal atmosphere of the primary school, but the secondary school teacher is also likely to have the additional problem of meeting some hundreds of pupils every week and hence to need an extremely streamlined recording system if assessment is not to become overwhelmingly time-consuming. In addition, the sheer size of the secondary school poses a communication problem which necessitates more formal and frequently a proliferation of record-keeping.

Just as diversity of curricula is likely to be a feature of the modern classroom in both primary and secondary schools, so is diversity of pupils. Some schools may find themselves coping with a high proportion of pupils representing a considerable diversity of ethnic groups, with all that this implies in terms of varying cultures and attitudes. Language, in particular, is likely to be a problem since it will be necessary for the teacher to have some ready means of monitoring varying levels of difficulty in this respect and subsequent progress. If, as is not infrequently the case, this heterogeneous classroom is further characterised by team teaching and, possibly, an open plan layout as well, the possibility of disorganisation, of individual children 'slipping through the net', of a non-cumulative approach to learning, is further increased and the necessity for a shared and systematic recording procedure becomes even more paramount.

It is clear that the end of term class test is singularly inappropriate for this kind of teaching situation as is the traditional list of grades in a markbook. But if new curricular and pedagogic approaches have revolutionised a good many of our classrooms, bringing with them an associated need for new assessment techniques founded on a quite different assessment philosophy, they have not done away with the need for the more comparable and formal grading of pupils which, for the present at least, must still be provided for certain school purposes. This, as we have seen, is likely to give rise to all sorts of contradictions, contradictions which are inherent in the frequently conflicting teaching and selection roles of the school. Once again, this problem is likely to be less immediate in the primary school, where selection is least pressing. Thus, in our attempt to begin to reconcile some of these contradictions, we shall look first at a primary school; at the various kinds of information the classroom teacher needs to record and some of the procedures which were developed in one school to meet these needs.

Recording in the primary classroom

Recent research[1] reveals a fairly wide variation in primary school assessment and reporting practices. In many schools checklists to record topics covered are used in maths and English. In some cases grades are used. Many use formal, standardised tests such as the Schonell word-recognition and reading tests, NFER tests of English, Neale Analysis or Richmond tests. Some keep more-or-less private records of personal development and home circumstances. Some provide formal reports to parents and/or secondary schools, some do not. For most teachers, day-to-day records are idiosyncratic notes and comments and reminders in relation to specific pupils' progress and future activities. Some teachers keep these 'working notes' in their heads; others have a book which is an integral part of their practice but of little use for any systematic recording of progress to be shared with colleagues or parents.

At Hilltop Primary School a great deal of time, effort and thought goes into designing and using records. This reflects the school's awareness of the importance of 'keeping track of teaching' and in many ways underpins its success in putting into practice a progressive educational philosophy and an open plan building — a degree of success which may be judged by its being chosen to be visited by a recent Secretary of State for Education.

In its booklet to parents, the school makes it clear that it puts strong emphasis on the 'vehicle'[2] subjects of English and maths and on the 'tapestry' subjects such as science, art, social studies, and the environment which are largely incorporated into the 'integrated studies' work which occupies up to half of the timetable.

Language

Language policies are the responsibility of the deputy head who has drawn up a variety of different records which serve to integrate the provision of a syllabus and the recording of individual progress. Some of these records, such as the 'Early Reading Games' checklist (Figure 2.1) and the 'Phonics Record', of which extracts are shown here, simply record a child's mastery of various parts of the syllabus such as being able to recite the alphabet, or of games involving particular reading skills such as vowel-recognition.

The lists of games is roughly ordered in terms of the various stages of developing reading skill and so can provide an easily interpretable 'record' for the teacher both in terms of the curriculum — topics

23

covered — and pupil progress — topics mastered. The provision of several columns allows several attempts at a game and their results to be recorded as a further aid to diagnosis of areas of difficulty.

CHILD'S NAME			DATE OF BIRTH				
		1st check	2nd check	3rd check	4th check		
1 Visual discrimination — matching							
2 Visual discrimination — completing shapes							
3 Visual discrimination — picture, shape sorting							
28 Positional word/picture matching							
29 Classification							
30 Question and answer (jigged)							
31 Sentence completion (no pictures)							

Figure 2.1   Early Reading Games (extract)

The 'Phonics Record' is essentially similar except it is the detailed skills concerned rather than merely the topic or the game that are quite explicitly identified, for example:

Alphabet — can recite with teacher alternating letters
           can recite saying 3 letters each
           can recite teacher 2 letter child 3
           teacher recites alphabet missing out letters

The overall Language Record is similar except that it is a profile in which 'spoken language' is broken down into 'speech', 'use of speech', 'listening and recording', and 'written language' into 'writing', 'conventions', 'use of writing', 'reading', 'using books and 'advanced writing' skills. Once again, several columns provide for repeated assessments. In practice, all these records are filled in, where appropriate, at least every half-term. The specific items under each of the headings, however, vary in the amount of judgment they require of the teacher in deeming whether the child has successfully mastered them. Thus 'has speech difficulty' is open to a good deal of variation in that what may be termed a difficulty to one teacher may not to another. Even more specific descriptions, such as 'can show a visitor round', or 'tells a story', are still relative in contrast to much more specific items like 'listens and responds correctly to instructions', 'all letters closed

24

CHILD'S NAME_____ DATE OF BIRTH_____

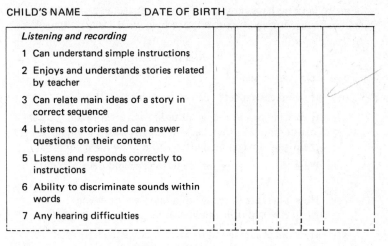

Listening and recording

1 Can understand simple instructions

2 Enjoys and understands stories related by teacher

3 Can relate main ideas of a story in correct sequence

4 Listens to stories and can answer questions on their content

5 Listens and responds correctly to instructions

6 Ability to discriminate sounds within words

7 Any hearing difficulties

Figure 2.2   Language Record (extract)

correctly' or 'knows at sight 100 most used words'.

In addition to recording pupils' developing skills in this way, the school feels it is important to record pupils' own interests and abilities as expressed in the extent and nature of their own individual reading. Thus there is also a 'Reading Record', which relates to the colour-coded reading scheme in which books appropriate to each level of reading (roughly associated with an age group) are classified under particular colours — green (5-6), black (6-7), brown (7-8), yellow (8-9), red (9-10), blue (10-11), white (11+). Not only does this provide a very easy guide for the teacher, it is an incentive for the pupil.

CHILD'S NAME_____ DATE OF BIRTH_____

Colour	Title	Date Started	Date Completed	Comments	Teacher

Figure 2.3   Reading Record

25

Finally, and perhaps most unusually, language assessment at Hilltop includes a teacher evaluation sheet, of which we show an extract.

WRITING – SOME QUESTIONS

(i)   Why was it set?

(ii) How much was set? (Can too much be set?)

(iii) How wide was the range of tasks? (e.g. recording, planning, instructing, informing, advising, persuading, arguing, theorising, imagining, writing from known experience)

(iv) Were the tasks appropriate to the age and development of the child?

(v)   How wide was the range of audiences for which the child wrote? Would other audiences be possible or helpful?

(vi) How did you respond to what was written? To what features did you mainly pay attention?

(vii) What help did you give during drafting?

(viii) How did you help at the pre-drafting stage?

(ix) What help do children give each other in drafting and editing work?

(x)   What are "reasonable" expectations in the current conventions of written language?

The 'writing questions' are accompanied by lists of suggested activities for writing which not only further encourage teachers to think about their objectives, but provide practical suggestions of suitable activities such as:

Tape small groups of children talking about their writing before they hand it in to the teacher. What will their discussion tell us about their perception of the writing task and of our priorities?

Collect the best 150 words of written work by a small sample of pupils each term. Review. What are the signs of development? What action needs to be taken?

It is clear that this question sheet will encourage teachers to think carefully about the various writing activities which they set pupils in terms of how each activity contributes to the development of different aspects of writing skill and why individual pupils may be having difficulties. As such, these 'writing questions' reflect Hilltop's recognition of the need for teachers in informal classrooms to make explicit the kinds of evaluative questions which more or less implicitly provide for the continuous process of decision-making that underpins any teaching situation. It is equally apparent, though, that although the need for this sort of questioning may be less apparent in the traditional 'class' room, its value for diagnostic and evaluative purposes is just as great.

Hilltop's emphasis on 'trouble-shooting' does not only cover writing. An even clearer emphasis on the diagnosis of problems is evident in the areas of reading and spelling, in which specific problems are matched against suitable methods of treatment. See, for example, Table 2.1.

TABLE 2.1   *Some common difficulties and suitable methods of treatment (extract)*

Symptoms	Useful methods of treatment
Mispronunciation. Confusion of similar consonants or vowels	Speech training. Lists of similar words given (a) orally (b) visually. Practice in recognising letters heard and seen. Training in analysis of words.
Reversals	Emphasis on direction of reading by exercises involving tracing, finger pointing, or underlining while reading.
Repetitions	Training in methods of attacking new words. Encouragement of calmness and slower rate. Reading aloud along with the pupils.

Thus, as far as the teaching of language skills at Hilltop is concerned, 'keeping track of teaching' is provided for by profiles of individual pupil development in all the different aspects of language activity, reinforced by the provision of questions and suggestions about the various kinds of learning activity involved in encouraging such development.

Mathematics

As might be expected, arrangements for recording progress in mathematics are similar, if less extensive, as shown in Figure 2.4. This record has since been replaced by a less detailed record since it proved too unwieldy.

NAME: AGE 1 Sept. 19   CLASS

Number	Addition			Facts				
	Subtraction			Facts				
	Multiplication			Facts				
	Division			Facts				
	Number Families	Odd Even	Prime	Square		Trian-gular	100 Square	Positive Negative
	Place value and multibase work			Ability to approximate				
				Probability				
				Averages				
	Fractions and operations with them			Percentages				
				Factors				
				Multiples				
	Decimal fractions ext. of base ten work			Ratio				
				Punch Cards				
				Equality				
	General comment							

Figure 2.4   Mathematics Record Sheet

In this record the criteria for whether or not the pupil has mastered a particular area are much more open to the teacher's discretion since specific tasks are not identified. The mathematics record is essentially concerned with identifying topics covered or skills mastered. There is little 'diagnostic' component built in which could help the teacher to discover why a pupil is not achieving mastery of a particular area. It is obvious, however, that such records which allow individual progress through, and mastery of, various parts of the syllabus to be recorded are a very much more sophisticated second cousin to the record of syllabus items covered *by the class as a whole* kept by most teachers concerned with whole class teaching.

Integrated studies

Up to half of each week is spent at Hilltop on integrated studies. Each child chooses a topic which he or she will pursue in a mixed age and ability group for half a term. The topics are designed by individual teachers in each of the major groupings of the school. 'Upper primary', or 'lower middle', for example, are offered a number of different topics each half-term for all the pupils in that section. The topics are carefully planned to incorporate a variety of the different traditional subject areas such as history, geography, science and religious education, which are all woven into areas of study such as 'wood', 'the seasons', 'fashion', or 'the Wild West'. Pupils decide the order in which they will tackle the work set and often work for quite long periods unsupervised whilst another room may contain two or three teachers working together.

Lower Middle Group   Hilltop Primary School
Autumn Term

Integrated Studies Topic: Autumn NAME	Poem	Leaf-prints	Weather	Story	Nature walk	Leaf mould	Hallowe'en	Trees	
Jane Adams	√			(Spelling) X	√	√	√		
Ann Brooks							√		
Michael Cole	√	√		√			√		
Fiona Gordon	X	√					√		
Philip Holmes							√		

Figure 2.5   Topic Record (extract)

The need for records is obviously central in a situation where teachers are involved with different pupils every half-term and pupils have a good deal of choice as to the order in which they will undertake the different parts of a topic. In practice, record-keeping takes a variety of more-or-less systematic forms ranging from the day-to-day conversations between the teachers, the regular weekly planning and evaluation meetings, the Topic Record (Figure 2.5) and the General Record (Figure 2.6). The Topic Record, as Figure 2.5 shows, is similar to other Hilltop records in being designed to record the parts of the syllabus covered successfully by each pupil.

The teacher can see at a glance from this sheet those parts of the topic successfully completed for each individual ($\sqrt{}$), those that still need attention in that they have not been adequately carried out (X), and those activities for which no entry is made which have not yet been tackled, by individual pupils, or, if the teacher is not yet ready to introduce them, the class as a whole.

Although a teacher may occasionally identify a particular problem on the record which is consistently causing trouble for an individual pupil, by and large record-keeping in integrated studies is like mathematics, oriented to recording work covered. The record has very limited value for identifying individual problems and even less for suggesting how they may be overcome. Equally, it does not identify outstanding interests or talents worthy of particular attention by the teacher. Part of the reason for this is that the recording emphasis is on activities covered rather than the underlying skills and attributes embodied in those activities.

The General Record

By contrast, the 'General Record' (Figure 2.6) puts great emphasis on skills. Indeed, this record, which is completed for each curricular area each term, is quite markedly different from the other Hilltop records in two other ways. First, it is based on a five-point scale and thus is virtually the only record to contain an element of comparison between pupils rather than mastery of particular curricular tasks. Second, it provides for the assessment of work-related behaviour and attitudes.

Thus, the general record provides a very comprehensive on-going profile of the pupil's development in comparison to other pupils in his or her group, a profile which will culminate in the recommendations made to the receiving secondary school. Such a record is also very important in providing information to a new school when a pupil's family moves in order that the receiving school can have a somewhat

Please use 5 point scale only

Curricular Area: Integrated Studies

Summer

E/S STUDY GROUP

NAME	Attitude	Initiative	Motivation	Co-operation (with staff)	Co-operation (with other children)	Written work (practical)	Written work (accuracy)	Practical work	Diagrams (and other pictorial work)	Art/craft attitude	Art/craft achievement
Denise Adams	C	C	C	C	C	D	C	B	C	D	C
Helen Brooks	A	B	A	B	C	B	C	B	C	A	A
Michael Carver	E	E	D	E	D	E	E	C	E	E	D
Ann Griggs	C	D	C	B	B	C	C	E	C	D	C
Peter Hall	B	C	B	C	B	C	C	C	B	C	C

Figure 2.6   Lower Middle Group, Hilltop Primary School: General Record

more objective picture of the *standard* of work the pupil has produced in the past.

Such is the more traditional stuff of reports, an approach which is familiar at Old Normgrade Grammar and which some of the parents at Hilltop would like to see incorporated in a formal term or year report, for at present they must come personally to the school if they would like guidance on their child's progress – a reflection of the school's individualist philosophy.

Comment

We have dawdled a long time in the colourful corners and spaces of Hilltop Primary. We are attracted by its cheerful informality and air of purpose; the freedom which is the prerogative of the primary school, not burdened with the harsh external realities of examinations, employment opportunities and the equally real internal traumas caused as adolescent pupils endeavour to realise an identity. You may feel we have spent too long at Hilltop, since its problems and solutions cannot be extended to very different sorts of schools. But you would be wrong. The only difference is that the integrated day, the open plan classroom, the individualised curriculum – all of which are almost exclusively primary school innovations – have forced teachers at this level to give creative and careful consideration to how and why they need to collect information about pupils' progress. In this way they highlight needs which are only now being recognised, needs which pertain to all classrooms if teachers are genuinely to 'keep track of teaching'. What, then, are these needs that the record system at Hilltop has been designed to meet?

Lessons to be learned from Hilltop

First, and most obvious, is the need to record the achievements of each child in relation to the various parts of a syllabus. Equally obviously, however, there is a good deal of confusion in the various records between merely keeping track of work done and the more difficult task of identifying specific strengths and weaknesses. Even when such a diagnosis has taken place, there remains the still more sensitive task of identifying the underlying cause of such tendencies prior to taking appropriate action in providing the most suitable kinds of learning experience. The teachers at Hilltop feel their recording system tends to fail to identify children at either end of the ability spectrum in need of such specific remedial help or extra stimulation. A more careful look at their records might also suggest that many children in the 'middle' need help with some aspects of their learning and need to be 'stretched' on other occasions.

It is clear that the teachers at Hilltop have recognised that curriculum and assessment must be integrally related in any teaching and learning situation that is intended to relate to the needs of the individual child. This is why we have chosen to contrast Hilltop with Old Normgrade in order to define the scope of this book. Yet recognising the need alone cannot solve the problem. New techniques of assessment are required to provide for teaching strategies to be chosen in relation to individual pupil learning characteristics. In chapter 3 we discuss some suitable approaches, most of which have been themselves developed by teachers, and look at this same problem being tackled in a secondary school context.

There are other stages in the individualised recording of pupil progress which equally are recognised at Hilltop, namely the need for a quick, efficient, easily accessible and cumulative record system. Having gathered detailed information about a pupil's learning for use in teaching, this information must be summarised and collated with assessments from other sorts of activity to provide a more concise and comprehensive picture of progress. This stage of assessment provides the sort of information needed to review progress — with parents, for example — but is equally important in determining whether learning patterns are a response to a particular activity or teacher or whether they are a more general characteristic. These sorts of needs will be the subject of chapter 5 and again we shall balance the experience of Hilltop with that of a secondary school to emphasise its applicability to *every sort of school*.

A third area of concern evident, if not emphasised, in Hilltop's records is a child's non-academic, personal and social development. Most teachers are concerned to foster such development and are supported in this by the majority of parents. Attitudes to learning, whether a child is lazy or enthusiastic, interested or bored, are closely related to achievement, and must be an integral part of any assessment programme oriented to providing appropriate learning situations for individual pupils. A child's relations with his peers, his teacher, his confidence and his behaviour are equally central, however. And if the modern progressive classroom makes this more obvious, it is not any less true for the teacher in the more traditional classroom if she wishes to do the best for each of her charges. In chapter 4 we look at some approaches to this kind of assessment, conscious that by so doing we enter an area which is both emotionally highly charged and morally controversial. Such a step is readily justified by the underlying rationale of the approach to assessment set out in this book: that any activity or aim deemed fit to constitute a goal of teaching automatically justifies the sensitive application of professional skills which can make those goals more readily realisable.

There is a fourth and final aspect of keeping track of teaching, at first sight the most simple, but at root one of the most difficult and controversial. It concerns how the information collected about a child as he or she moves up through the school should be consolidated into a form suitable to be conveyed to interested parties outside the school. At the primary school level, formal demands of this sort on the school are few since the typically smaller size of the school and close involvement of the pupil with one teacher makes individual parent-teacher interviews both feasible and desirable. If some yardstick of school performance is demanded, standardised test results can, as they do at Hilltop, satisfy outside interests that standards are being maintained. But the position of the secondary school is a great deal more difficult in this respect. Universities, employers, careers officers and parents demand a variety of information and often in a way which those in the school feel exerts an undesirable constraint on the curriculum. Public examinations in particular are often deplored in this respect. How are such demands to be reconciled in assessment procedures oriented to recognising individual pupil's interests and needs? Is it possible to retain the emphasis on mastery, so obvious at Hilltop, even at the secondary level? Such problems are the subject of chapter 6.

Every school and every classroom is unique. No two teachers have exactly the same teaching style. No two teachers would define their aims in precisely the same way. Equally, every assessment concern is specific to that particular constellation of personalities, ideals, and skills which together produce the very individual character of any school. Equally, though, there are experiences, needs and concerns which appear to be shared by all those teachers and schools who, either by force of circumstances or by conviction, are determined to make assessment the servant, rather than the master of teaching. It is for these schools and these teachers that the practical suggestions of this book are offered.

Chapter 3

Keeping track of learning

At Old Normgrade Grammar and Hilltop Primary, school assessment policy was our main focus of attention. But in fact the most important possibilities for using assessment to keep track of learning are not in the hands of school reporting systems, or even examination boards, but under the direct control of the teacher in his or her own classroom. The geography department of Broughton High School is an example of one which has taken the opportunity very seriously for, as readers who have persevered this far in the book will already be aware, one of the most powerful pressures underlying the need to develop new assessment procedures has been the widespread adoption of more individualised curricula. In some ways, at least, the class test is not an inappropriate adjunct to the class lesson. For mixed ability teaching based on graded work assignments, where students progress at their own pace, it is totally inappropriate. In many primary schools, like Hilltop, the replacement of such tests by different strategies has occasioned little mourning. In secondary schools, where much greater variation between the priorities of different subject departments may be expected, schoolwide initiatives are likely to be rare. This is the case at Broughton High School, where the geography department has decided to 'go it alone' in the development of novel teaching and assessment procedures.

New curricula: new assessment problems

The work of the department is organised into a series of well thought-out and largely self-contained modules, each of which takes about one month to teach. As in most progressive geography departments in secondary schools, there is an ample supply of resources and visual materials and much of the teaching is based on carefully planned

35

worksheets devised and written by the teachers themselves. The assessment system which went along with this teaching practice until two or three years ago also seemed fairly progressive. With the exception of a formal examination at the end of the second year, when decisions had to be made as to the most appropriate course for pupils to take in the following year, assessment was by continuous testing. This meant that at the end of each module the pupils were set a short test on everything they had learned in the previous month. The average mark on these continuous assessment tests over the period prior to issuing a report to parents was translated into a grade which seemed to satisfy everyone concerned.

The department came to achieve a worthwhile reputation, and it was hardly surprising that they were invited to participate in a national working party on mixed ability teaching in geography.[1] As a result of this involvement, the teachers began to feel that what they had up till then assumed to be a fairly satisfactory curriculum had glaring problems especially in their first- and second-year mixed ability classes.

The first problem was that the intended learning outcomes which they had set for each module of work were unrealistically complex for some pupils, and for others presented insufficient challenge. To overcome this they decided to specify a set of core intended outcomes which they hoped that all pupils would master, and a set of extension outcomes which would be the focus of learning for those pupils who had already attained the core.

The second problem arose directly from the decision to adopt a core/extension approach and to attempt to have all pupils attain the core. If these intentions were to be taken seriously, then the teacher had to find out as reliably as possible which pupils had attained the core before they devoted too much of their time to extension work. They also had to know which pupils had not attained particular elements of the core while there was still sufficient time to do something about it during the time allotted to teaching the unit. Now it was clear that the continuous assessment tests were not providing this information. On the one hand, they took place at the end of the module which left no time for remedial action. On the other, the test tended to investigate general attainment in the whole module and it was difficult to relate substantial parts of the test to individual core intended outcomes. In short, the tests were not designed to give information to pupils and teachers on their specific strengths and weaknesses. Continuous assessment was best described as a staccato form of the final examination.

A solution in diagnostic assessment

The solution adopted by the department was to initiate a programme of diagnostic assessment. It was decided that the first phase of the diagnostic procedure should consist of tests in which a small number of items or questions would reveal each individual core intended outcome. The second phase was to take place when the pupil attempted the remedial exercise and had an opportunity to discuss any problems he had with the teacher. These tests had to be brief enough to fit into the normal teaching sequence, yet sufficiently accurate to pick out those pupils who were having difficulties. Furthermore, when multiple choice tests or questions where guessing was possible were being used, it was felt that one item would not give a reliable indication of attainment, and so several similar items were used. Thus, if five items were being used to test for understanding of the concept 'depression' in a weather unit, the teachers decided that pupils answering any four or five of these items correctly had mastered the intended outcome and were able to move on to an extension exercise, while those who had answered less than four correctly were given an additional remedial exercise to reinforce their learning. As is shown in Figure 3.1, the outcome was that the department's assessment programme came to comprise a series of diagnostic tests distributed throughout each module. Each test contained a series of sub-tests and the information provided was a simple statement of whether or not each pupil had attained the mastery score on each of the intended outcomes.

Now, from an assessment viewpoint the most important thing to note is that in the geography department of Broughton High School, testing has become almost completely integrated with the teaching/learning process. The feedback provided by the test is required both by teacher and student to make important decisions on how best to move forward, and the information provided relates to the specific intentions of the course and not to 'general attainment' in geography, which so often hides the specific strengths and weaknesses of the student in the need to provide easily calculated grades for school reports. This alternative integrated and diagnostic approach has considerable potential for, and indeed may be said to be vital to, the modern classroom, and thus forms the focus of a substantial part of this book.

But what are the problems that may be encountered in changing to this style of assessment? Perhaps most important is that the staff should be committed to trying out the new idea. Sometimes external support services — curriculum developers or collaborative researchers — provide a useful impetus. However, when these transient change agents move on to pastures new it is not at all unusual for the innovations which they

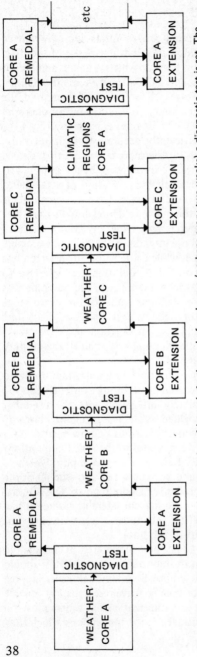

The learning sequence is divided into a series of 'cores'. At the end of each core (perhaps every two weeks) a diagnostic test is set. The outcome of this test indicates which parts of the core have not been mastered. Each pupil is then given remedial work on sections which have not been mastered, or if they have mastered the entire core they move on to extension work. An opportunity is also provided for pupils who have completed their remedial work to move on to extension.

Figure 3.1   Diagnostic assessment built into the teaching strategy

have encouraged to be put aside. Much more important for long-term change is the attitude of the individual teacher who will eventually carry the responsibility for accepting or rejecting the innovation. In this instance there was sufficient interest for what began as an experiment to become departmental policy.

Closely associated with the acceptance of an innovation is the time required to carry it through. This was a major problem in Broughton, but it was overcome by each member of the department taking responsibility for a module of work which allowed the innovation to be accommodated at the rate of one year-group per session. In addition, the lack of assessment resources available from outside the school was potentially one of the most serious obstacles to its widespread adoption.

Finally, the department's change in assessment procedures had to fit in with school policy as a whole. Broughton High School is no Old Normgrade, but there are tensions. At the time when this innovation took place, the school required regular grades from each department for reporting purposes.[2] But the feedback from the department's diagnostic assessment is not designed to be added up and averaged. Nor are the tests ideally taken by all students at the same time. They are far better tackled by each individual when he is ready for them. Does this mean that the teacher has to set two types of test for each unit? Is the diagnostic feedback to be ignored for reporting purposes? Such problems are of vital importance and are considered further in later chapters, 5 and 6.

The geography department of Broughton High offers a very important perspective on assessment. We have seen in chapter 1 that one of the basic reasons for assessment is to diagnose the problems which individual classes or individual pupils may have with particular elements of their learning. Typically, however, while most teachers recognise that tests have the potential to be diagnostic instruments, it is only exceptionally that a systematic procedure to find pupils' learning difficulties is the main focus of a school assessment policy, especially in secondary schools. The main reason for this is the overwhelming effect which reporting and external certification has on the curriculum – 'our national obsession with examining, testing, grading, cataloguing, pigeon-holing and stratifying'.[3]

Essentially, the teachers in Broughton High saw testing and teaching as inseparable and complementary elements in learning. This is similar to the view expressed by Glaser,[4] who suggests that:

Testing and teaching are inseparable aspects and not two different enterprises as one might be led to believe by current practices in education. Frequent information about student performance is used

39

as a basis on which the teacher decides on the next instructional step: and equally important it also serves as a feedback to the student. It is also invaluable data for the design and redesign of teaching materials.

While this view may not be far removed from that of the committed primary school teacher who sets regular spelling tests, individually evaluates her children to guide them through appropriate reading schemes and makes her pupils keep their own SRA progress cards, it is not all that common in the typical secondary school. And it is against this background that the pupil-centred diagnostic assessment policy used in the geography department of Broughton High is in most striking contrast. But, of course, there is nothing new in education, which means that we may be better placed to understand it by searching out existing traditions.

The child-centred tradition

The idea of basing the curriculum on individual needs is far from new, even if the use of a parallel and systematic assessment programme, which to a considerable extent has been brought about by the pressures of pupil-teacher ratios, was less prominent in earlier attempts. As long ago as the 1860s, when Charlotte Mason began her teaching career in the middle-class schools of Victorian England, we can find recognition of child-centred education as being something different from teacher-centred instruction. Charlotte Mason's philosophy was basically that the child did not need to learn everything through the teacher. Teacher-centred instruction left the student as the passive recipient of knowledge and because classes of students were forced to learn at the same rate, the teacher was not in a position to take account of the individual needs of her pupils. Similarly, in the United States the pioneering work of Helen Pankhurst, which came to be known as the 'Dalton Plan' after the school in Dalton, Massachusetts, where she worked, put tremendous emphasis on individual assignments where the student was directed to find the information for himself. The result, of course, was that each student came to produce large amounts of personal written material which led Taylor[5] to note that when the Dalton Plan was introduced in the UK, 'The convention that written work was always to be corrected, resulted in masters disappearing in a blizzard of paper' — a hazard that contemporary teachers would certainly wish to avoid!

These early attempts at child-centred education have their modern parallel in the primary school classroom, with its project work, integrated day and individual assignments based on pupil interest. Yet, as we saw in Hilltop School in chapter 2, the teacher with a typical class of more than thirty pupils faces considerable problems and requires novel solutions in keeping track of the individual's progress when such innovations are introduced. In secondary schools, however, the great corset of the certificate syllabus, and the pressures experienced by many teachers who may teach more than 250 different pupils every week, have been particularly significant in militating against the widespread uptake of such labour-intensive assessment as is necessitated by writing-oriented teaching strategies such as the Dalton Plan.

The criterion-referenced tradition

In the geography department of Broughton High School there is evidence too of a more systematic approach to diagnosing students' learning difficulties than is evident in the work of Mason, Pankhurst and their descendants. In particular, the emphasis put on diagnosing the difficulties experienced by individual pupils in attaining individual intended learning outcomes through a battery of carefully designed diagnostic procedures is worthy of special note. Particularly significant is the fact that these procedures are more precisely focused than the written reports upon which the Dalton Plan is based. These 'Criterion-Referenced Tests' give information on whether a student has mastered a particular element of learning and therefore place students in two sets — those who have attained the intended outcomes and those who have not. This is in contrast with the more familiar 'norm-referenced' tests which determine whether a student has learned the segment of knowledge better than his classmates and hence provides a list of pupils in rank order. Again, the initial interest in this approach can be traced back to a move from teacher-based instruction to individualised learning, but this time of a different order.

In the 1950s in the United States a psychologist called Skinner developed the idea of applying his work to the construction of teaching machines for programmed learning. A descendant of this initiative is the Texas Instruments 'Little Professor', which is a simple teaching machine used widely by children in their homes today. With this the child selects from four levels of difficulty and four arithmetic operations, and the machine supplies a random selection of problems such as $8 \times 4 = ?$, $11 \times 14 = ?$, and so on. If the child gives the correct response then the machine provides another problem. If the response is incorrect, the machine repeats the question until on the third incorrect response it provides the solution. At the end of each set of ten items the child's score for the set is provided.

Skinner's work in programmed learning substituted for the teacher-learner relationship a rigidly sequential series of learning tasks or 'frames'. This very rigidity as well as the generally poor student response to anything greater than short programmes contributed substantially to a fairly limited uptake of the notion except in specific practical training situations. Of much wider importance, however, was the awareness which grew up in the 1960s amongst American educationists working in programmed learning that the decisions which had to be made about a student's suitability for a given course, or his success in attaining its outcomes, depended on sound criterion-referenced assessment.

Contemporary practice

The great drawback of many of these earlier attempts to focus on the specific problems of individual children seems to have been, especially in the case of the Dalton Plan, the volume of work required. Skinner's programmed learning approach so depersonalised learning as to make it unpalatable except in small doses, but it did act as a catalyst to the development of criterion-referenced assessment.

The problem facing today's curriculum and assessment developer who wants this level of individual feedback in a normal classroom of thirty or more pupils, therefore, is to develop a system which focuses on the teacher's most important intended learning outcomes for a piece of work, and yet does not result in such a workload as to deter the teacher from using it, nor make the pupil feel that he has plugged into a machine. Some examples of how this has been attempted will illustrate the potential and the problems of such an approach.

Mastery learning

Perhaps the most widely researched approach to teaching using diagnostic assessment is 'mastery learning'. Amongst its main proponents is Benjamin Bloom, whose name is associated in the minds of most British teachers with the idea of taxonomies of objectives in the cognitive and affective domains. Equally, though, Bloom has pioneered in his research the idea that all pupils will make better progress if they attain mastery of the intended outcomes at each stage of their learning. In his account of mastery learning he states that:[6]

There are many versions of mastery learning at present. All begin with the notion that most students can attain a high level of learning capability if instruction is approached sensitively and systematically, *if students are helped when and where they have learning difficulties*, [author's italics] if they are given sufficient time to achieve mastery and if there is some clear criterion of what constitutes mastery.

The notion will be more easily explained after consulting Figure 3.2. In this simple model of school learning, the outcomes of the procedure through which we put our pupils in school are seen as being a function of the pupil's 'cognitive entry behaviour', which might loosely be described as his knowledge of whatever he needs to know before he begins a learning task (for example, the necessity that a pupil should know how to use a protractor before he is asked to construct a pie-graph) and his 'affective entry characteristics', which include his motivation to benefit from instruction. These 'pupil entry characteristics' are mediated through a series of learning tasks which will vary in suitability according to 'quality of instruction'. The learning outcomes of the process are then subdivided in the model to include the level and type of achievement, the rate of learning and affective outcomes.

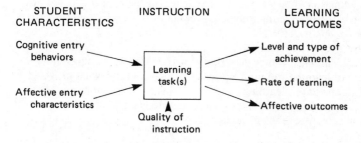

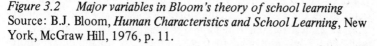

Figure 3.2   Major variables in Bloom's theory of school learning
Source: B.J. Bloom, *Human Characteristics and School Learning*, New York, McGraw Hill, 1976, p. 11.

Bloom pays considerable attention to the relationship between 'cognitive' and 'affective' entry characteristics and this takes us into the vital area of motivation. The determinants of motivation are extremely complex, having their roots in a child's very earliest experiences. However, the close relationship between assessment and motivation has long been recognised, and testing in one form or another has traditionally come to be used to encourage inter-pupil rivalry and competition, and hence motivation. Many teachers reading this book know only too well that this source of motivation is effective only for the relatively successful members of any particular group. For those pupils, often the majority, whose classroom experience is a continually reinforced feeling of failure, assessment is more likely to encourage a negative bravado, or passive opting out, than it is to encourage motivation. In this sense, all cognitive assessment is also non-cognitive. It has some effect on a pupil's self-image, his self-respect, his confidence, and hence his interest and his willingness to participate. Indeed, the traditional, almost exclusive predominance of academic assessment has led to academic evaluations being translated in the pupil's mind into how much the teacher values him personally.

The assessment procedures involved in mastery learning offer an alternative to this as one of the ways in which learning can become more intrinsically satisfying to a pupil, as it is less related to some comparative criteria, and more to the evaluation of his progress in relation to specific expected outcomes, or indeed to his own personally evolved goals.

However, it is the 'quality of the instruction' element in the model which has most relevance to our current interest. Research by Bloom and his associates suggests that if students are given feedback and remedial help over a series of learning tasks, and if each student is given time to master the essential pre-requisites for the next sequential learning task, then the result will be in keeping with Bloom's central mastery learning construct that:

> Most students become very similar with regard to learning ability, rate of learning and motivation for further learning when provided with favourable learning conditions. This research questions . . .
> the necessary permanence of such traits as good/poor learning ability or fast/slow learning characteristics.

The two most important variables in the 'quality of instruction' were found to be the presence of appropriate feedback and remedial procedures at each vital stage in pupil learning, and the extent to which pupils could be motivated to take advantage of them. Furthermore, although Bloom and his associates have tried to use a variety of feedback processes, including workbooks, quizzes, homework, etc., they found that brief diagnostic tests designed to determine what each pupil had learned, or failed to learn, were the most useful, and, in turn, that 'The efficiency of the correctives and the additional time needed are direct functions of the quality of the diagnostic-progress feedback testing.'

Clearly, then, in mastery learning we have an approach to the whole process of teaching, learning and assessment which has many parallels with the exploratory work we have described at Broughton High. The special importance of Bloom's work, however, is that his strategies have been tried, researched and developed over a considerable number of years. This has allowed Bloom and his associates to arrive at a number of important conclusions. These include:

1 The use of mastery learning techniques can result in 80 per cent of pupils in a class attaining the same standard as the top 20 per cent of pupils taught by the same teacher using non-mastery techniques.
2 If the approach is used by teachers in most subjects, pupils spend more of their classroom time on active learning, become more able to diagnose their own learning problems and develop the skill of seeking out help.
3 The pupil is likely to have more interest in learning because frequent evidence of success will improve his self-confidence as a learner.
4 There may be long-term benefits in mental health as there is evidence that repeated success in schools over a number of years increases the likelihood that an individual can withstand stress and anxiety in later life.

Clearly, the implications of adopting a mastery learning approach to teaching are considerable, not least in the time that must be allotted, at least in the initial stages, to allowing as many pupils as possible to master each learning task before moving on to the next one. Nor, indeed, has the thorny problem of what the other pupils should be doing while some are engaged in remedial work been fully answered. However, the clear value of focusing assessment on diagnostic tests related to the specific intended outcomes of a unit of learning cannot be underestimated.

As yet mastery learning is not a widely used teaching strategy in British schools. Despite Bloom's assertions that the difference in the time which pupils of different initial 'entry characteristics' take to attain successive pieces of learning diminishes substantially as they progress through the course, there are nevertheless implications which provide obstacles to most British teachers' uptake of the notion. Perhaps most significant is that time must be available in the system to allow some pupils to progress substantially while others work on the core. The notion of 'extension' work which we noted in Broughton is not well developed in most of the mastery learning literature and one is left wondering what the 'masters' are supposed to do with their time.

Needless to say, however, the notion of criterion-referenced diagnostic evaluation of progress with remedial help is neither new nor

45

unique to mastery learning. In particular, the approach is central to much good teaching practice where the teacher talks to individual pupils about their learning difficulties, or where she makes comments on specific aspects of an essay or a piece of project work. However, it is very unusual, not least because of the time required, for a teacher to work her way systematically through the whole class, searching out problems and prescribing remedial help. Furthermore, when written work is being marked, the teacher's comments seldom refer systematically to the range of intended learning outcomes which might be the reason for setting the topic, but tend rather to chance on idiosyncratic aspects of the pupil's writing. Now while this may be an excellent means of giving feedback to the pupils on their ability to communicate in written English, or their capacity to argue logically and consistently, it does not give them information on the more subject specific aspects of their work. However, especially in recent years, a number of curriculum packages have been developed which incorporate a more systematic application of criterion-referenced assessment as an aid to learning.

Tour de France

A recent attempt to apply this basic principle has been used in the 'Tour de France' course developed by a working party in Scotland.[7] The course is designed to cover French in the first two years of secondary school. It is divided into a number of themes such as 'Paris', 'French houses', 'the Alps' and 'clothes', each of which is further divided into a number of topics.

The course focuses on the development of oral and aural communication skills rather than the grammar and written work of more traditional modern language teaching. Furthermore, it is an important underlying assumption that *all* pupils in the first two years of secondary school should be able to attain worthwhile levels of performance in French, rather than French lessons being an opportunity for some to develop increasing fluency, while others develop increasing despondency and a negative attitude to foreign languages in general.

There are a number of intriguing aspects to Tour de France. From a curriculum point of view, the wealth and breadth of materials available is well up to the standard of contemporary course packages. Second, the intended outcomes of pupil learning for each unit are clearly stated. Thus, for example, in theme one (Paris), the expected outcomes are stated not only in terms of content, such as 'family life', 'the school' and so on, but also in the form of the communication behaviours which the pupils have been taught.

46

Some objectives from 'Tour de France'

These objectives are stated on the pupil's report card for parents

A ASPECTS OF LIFE IN FRANCE

Theme 1 is based in Paris and covers the following aspects of life there:
1 Family life
2 Life in a new suburb
3 The school
4 Tourist Paris

B WHAT ALL PUPILS HAVE SO FAR BEEN TAUGHT TO DO (COMMUNICATIVE OBJECTIVES)

1 Giving personal information
2 Meeting and leaving people
3 Asking/Saying how people are
4 Asking/Saying who it is
5 Asking for food/drink at table
6 Handing over food/drink at table
7 Offering food/drink at table
8 Refusing/Accepting/Thanking at table
9 Discussing the time
10 Giving commands
11 Asking/Saying what something is
12 Expressing a range of personal feelings
13 Asking about/Expressing likes, dislikes, preferences
14 Showing someone round
15 Asking/Saying how much something costs
16 Asking/Saying who something is for
17 Asking/Saying how many there are
18 Asking/Saying what something is
19 Asking/Saying how to get to a place

The stated aim of making the course a valuable learning opportunity for all pupils is more than a pious hope. Built into the resources for each topic are two diagnostic tests, one for comprehension and another for listening and speaking. The comprehension test is typically an aural test of twenty to thirty items related to the specific objectives of the topic and the pupils are expected to attain a score of not less than 80 per cent for 'mastery'. A number of strategies can be used in applying the test including setting aside a 'testing' period when everyone takes

47

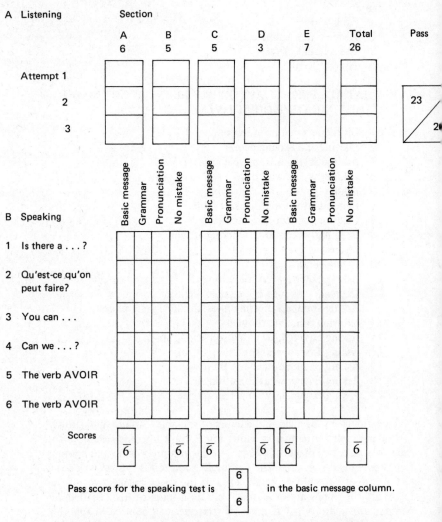

Figure 3.3   Diagnostic checksheet for a unit in 'Tour de France'

the whole test, testing a few pupils each period and, perhaps most satisfactory, although posing the most complex managerial problems, allowing individual pupils to take the test when they feel ready for it.

The listening and speaking diagnostic test for each topic is based on a five- to ten-minute 'mini interview' between individual pupils and the teacher, with each pupil utterance being monitored under the headings Content (is the pupil getting the basic message across); Form (is the pupil's response grammatically accurate); and Pronunciation (not necessarily up to the standard of a native speaker). The diagnostic checksheet for the 'arrivée à l'hotel' topic is shown in Figure 3.3.

Now there are two important points to make about both of these diagnostic tests. First, the content of the test is very closely related to the specific objectives of the course being taught, and so the teacher is able to interpret the outcome, not in terms of general attainment in French, which is the way in which school tests are typically treated, but rather within the more specific construct of mastery of specific subject skills or knowledge. They thus fall into the broad category of criterion-referenced tests. Second, the outcomes of the test provide information on which the teacher (or the pupil) can make decisions about short-term differentiated work. Those who have mastered the content of the test will move on to extension work which might involve them in performing other activities such as writing or reading in French. Those whom the test indicates not to have mastered the content can be given further remedial work on the crucial components of the course which will prepare them better to enter the subsequent unit with a more thorough knowledge of the basics. Thus the diagnostic and the remedial/ extension component of the course gives individual pupils the opportunity to progress at their own rate and so provides meaningful learning opportunities for all pupils.

At the end of each theme, i.e. every twelve to fourteen weeks, an *attainment* test is also provided which tests the additional ability of long-term retention, although it is again largely a listening and speaking test. The outcome of these attainment tests form the basis for the course report card (Figure 3.4) which comments on pupil attainment at basic and more complex levels. The recipient is also given a list of learning outcomes to which the report refers, and the criteria which are used to allot pupil attainment to the various categories.

Tour de France is thus a curriculum package into which both diagnostic tests and a reporting system have been built. Its restriction, which in many cases may also be its strength, is that it is highly prescriptive and thus gives the teacher less room for manoeuvre.

Keeping track of learning

School: .... Name: .... Class: ....

NATIONAL S1/S2 FRENCH PROJECT (SCOTLAND)

TOUR DE FRANCE

REPORT CARD: THEMES 1–3

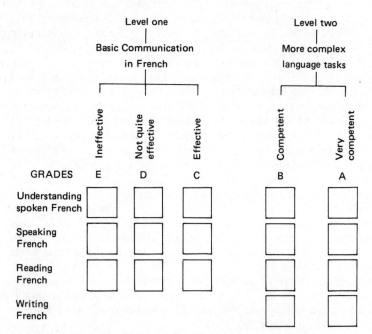

It is worth mentioning here that a GRADE C, indicating *effective basic communication* in French, may represent for many children a worthwhile achievement in French and will mean that they can achieve real communication with native speakers of French within the range of purposes specified overleaf in Section B.

Comment by class teacher

1   Present attainment
2   Effort/attitude
3   Future potential

Teacher: .... Parent/Guardian: ....

Date: .... Date: ....

RC 1/3–

Figure 3.4   Pupil report card for part of 'Tour de France'

50

TABLE 3.1   *Criteria used to allot pupils to 'Levels of Achievement' in reports from 'Tour de France'*

LEVELS OF ATTAINMENT IN BASIC COMMUNICATION IN FRENCH

	Effective communication	Highly effective communication
Understanding spoken French	Able to understand at least 70% of the information given in several short passages of French based on the above-mentioned communicative objectives.	Able to understand at least 90% of the information given in several short passages of French based on the above-mentioned communicative objectives.
Speaking French	Able to express the above communicative objectives in utterances that, though containing mistakes in grammar and pronunciation, are still clearly comprehensible to a native speaker of French.	Able to express the above communicative objectives with a good French pronunciation and a high degree of grammatical accuracy.

A particularly interesting aspect of these relatively straightforward criteria is that they are reported to parents as part of the report card (Figure 3.4).

The Diagnostic Assessment Project

A slightly different approach to the materials-oriented assessment procedures of Tour de France can be found in recent teacher-based work such as that of the Diagnostic Assessment Project of the Scottish Council for Research in Education. As in Broughton High School, assessment is not related to a piece of curriculum development. Instead, groups of teachers in a number of subjects, including geography, technical education, home economics and modern languages, have tried to develop, with the help of the research team, diagnostic tests and instruments which are directly applicable to their own existing schemes of work. A model for the creation of a teaching and assessment strategy involving diagnostic principles evolved from the work of the Project and this is illustrated in Figure 3.5.

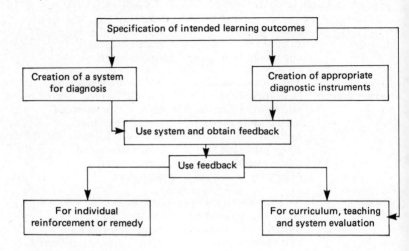

Figure 3.5   A model for the creation of diagnostic systems

The first stage requires the teacher to clarify his intentions for his course. The teachers' handbook[8] which has been published as one of the outcomes of the Project, stresses at considerable length the range of intended outcomes on which a teacher might decide to focus his diagnostic assessment. Furthermore, it is emphasised that unless the choice of elements of learning or 'domains' is chosen carefully and with special regard to the whole range of possible learning outcomes, there is danger of distorting the curriculum. A similar argument has been put forward by Wilhelms,[9] who suggests that:

> In recent years valuable new programmes of science and mathematics have been "sold" on their ability to get away from rote memorisation and manipulation, to create a new spirit of enquiry and sense of discovery, to build a new level of divergent thought and creativity. Yet if the measures used to evaluate them do not themselves highlight these great values — if they regress to the old narrow emphasis — then it is a cinch that the programmes too will regress.

Designing a diagnostic assessment system

It might be a criticism of the work carried out in Broughton which is described above that the emphasis was very much on cognitive attainment in geography and, indeed, in subsequent work in other units, the department came to diagnose pupil success in for example, creative writing, use of language, personal characteristics and attitude change towards the problems of the Third World.

The next two stages in the model, which comprise the creation of diagnostic tests and instruments and devising systems for diagnosis, are complementary. Obviously diagnostic tests must be created, but there is little value in tapping such a rich resource of information on pupil attainment in specific parts of the course unless a system has been devised which will allow this information to be collected and used efficiently.

Taking the creation of a system for diagnosis first, it is very important for the teacher to be aware that there is not a single prescriptive way in which diagnostic assessment should be carried out. Essentially, two points have to be considered. The first concerns the efficient accumulation and recording of the outcomes of the diagnosis, because in many cases the traditional markbook kept by teachers is a cumbersome and inefficient means of building up a clear diagnostic profile. The solutions devised by different departments are typically varied, but two are worthy of special note. Figure 3.6 shows a record sheet which was devised by a modern languages department to deal with the problem of keeping a longitudinal record of pupil progress in a number of areas. Both the pupils and the teacher were able to keep copies of this record, and a clear indication of parts of the course in which a pupil was having problems was immediately available throughout the year.

In a home economics department the problems were seen to be different. The pupil was required to master certain basic skills in the use of the sewing machine before the teacher was content to allow them to use the machines without immediate supervision. The analogy with driving tests was clear, and the department devised a 'driving licence' (Figure 3.7) to certify proficiency in each of a number of sewing machine skills. The certificate had the dual benefit of helping the teachers to record pupil achievement of at least a minimum level of competence in the necessary skills, and being highly motivating to pupils in offering readily achievable goals. The idea has now spread to other departments in the school, such as maths, which issues its own 'calculator driving licence'.

The second basic concern in designing a system is to decide where to incorporate the diagnostic tests. In most school assessments the test is

Class: ...2G1... Teacher: ...Mrs. Smart..........................

Unit		NAME Jimmy McPhail 1 2 3 4 5 6 7 8	NAME Sadie Wright 1 2 3 4 5 6 7 8	NAME Edna Everage 1 2 3 4 5 6 7 8	NAME 1 2 3 4 5 6 7 8
Aural Comprehension	1 2 3 4 5				
Written Comprehension	1 2 3 4 5				
Vocabulary & Structural Specifics	1 2 3 4 5				
Structures in context	1 2 3 4 5				
Lab. Imitation	1 2 3 4 5				
Lab. Question and Answer	1 2 3 4 5				
Written work in class	1 2 3 4 5				
Oral work in class	1 2 3 4 5				
Concentration in class	1 2 3 4 5				
Homework	1 2 3 4 5				

Figure 3.6   The diagnostic profile recording sheet used in a modern languages department
Source: H.D. Black and W.B. Dockrell, *Diagnostic Assessment in Secondary Schools*, Edinburgh, Scottish Council for Research in Education, 1980.

54

WESTER HAILES DRIVING LICENCE

NAME [   ]   CLASS [   ]

SIGNATURE [   ]

This person named is hereby licensed to drive a Viking Husqvarna Automatic
Sewing Machine

He/She is therefore able to:

TASK	On completion tick here
(1) Carefully take out and prepare for use	
(2) Fill a spool	
(3) Thread up machine correctly	
(4) Stitch a straight-line	
(5) Reverse for 5 cms	
(6) Sew a zig-zag line	
(7) Stitch a curved line	
(8) Stitch a straight-line and turn a corner	
(9) Replace a broken needle with a new one	
(10) Pack up machine and replace in box	

Sign on completion of above work

STUDENT:_____

*Figure 3.7   A 'driving licence' assessment record sheet in home
economics*

55

applied at the end of a given unit of work. Feedback is then delayed until the test is marked, which is normally well into the next unit. Where, as in the modern language system shown above, the intended outcomes are typically longitudinal, this may not pose great problems as the potential for remedy and reinforcement is in the work of the then current unit. However, where the intended outcomes are discrete to the particular unit of work, as was the case in our Broughton study, then any misunderstanding must be remedied within the time-span of that unit, and so the traditional approach is inappropriate.

The solution adopted by the Broughton Geography department was shown in Figure 3.1, but it would be wrong to assume that there is a 'diagnostic assessment model' which is an alternative to the traditional system. Instead, it is up to individual teachers to use diagnostic tests and instruments where they fit most appropriately into their own teaching strategy.

The means of diagnosing pupils' attainment of intended outcomes can include a wide variety of kinds of tests and instruments — multiple choice tests, essays, observation schedules, oral and aural tests. The two essential features of good diagnostic tests are, first, that they relate to areas or 'domains' of knowledge which are both manageable and appropriate, and, second, that they test what they set out to test — that they are 'content valid'.

To take the issue of the nature of the domain tested, it is worth thinking about the example of a physics teacher who is creating a test for a unit of work on 'electricity'. In the traditional approach he designs a test which samples his pupils' understanding of the fairly wide domain of concepts, skills and knowledge associated with electricity. However, when he wants to investigate the pupil's understanding of the concepts 'resistance', 'voltage' and 'ohm', then he is sampling within much more specific domains where general attainment in electricity and test scores are of little value. The problem at this stage is one of balance. Too many objectives at this stage create logistic difficulties in creating the tests and acting on the information. At the same time, as we have noted already, specifying only those intended outcomes which are easy to assess can result in a distorted curriculum.

The second important issue is whether the tests or instruments investigating the domain are 'content valid'. Content validity addresses the question 'Does this item (exclusively) test the specific intended learning for which it was designed?' Clearly, unless the items are content valid it will be impossible to draw a valid inference from the results and so the whole process will become pointless. It is worth noting that if they are to be successful, diagnostic tests require rather more care in their construction than the typical 'general attainment' test, although as we have seen in our case studies above, when they are written well they provide invaluable information for both teacher and pupil alike.

Having designed and implemented a diagnostic system, the next stage is obviously to *use* the information provided. The first potential use is that a teacher can investigate which of his intended outcomes are being attained by a large proportion of his pupils, and which are proving difficult for the class as a whole. From this the teacher can reconsider his objectives and teaching strategies for that particular year-group or class of pupils. Second, information is provided about which *pupils* are failing to attain particular concepts, skills or elements of knowledge. The teacher can use this information to differentiate his teaching, to provide reinforcement or remedy work for the pupils with problems, and extension work for pupils who have successfully attained each element of the core. Thus, all pupils are in a position to receive both positive and negative feedback from the tests. This has the predictable impact on their motivation.

It is clear from the foregoing that diagnostic assessment is a generalisable approach which has potential in a wide variety of subjects and teaching situations since it allows the teacher to pace her teaching either to the progress of the class as a whole or to each individual pupil, depending on her approach. Equally, whatever the subject and the teaching style, pupils need to know how they are getting on in different aspects of a subject in order to build on their strengths and try and overcome areas of difficulty. Where a teacher is committed to a more individualised pedagogy — either by choice or as a result of the organisational situation in which she finds herself — such as mixed ability classes — the need for diagnostic assessment becomes even more imperative as the experience of Broughton High School testifies.

Pupil self-assessment

The essential notion behind diagnostic assessment is that it will help both the teacher and the pupil to become more aware of areas of learning which have not yet been mastered. Most good teachers will be aware of parts of their course which they feel that many or some of their pupils have had difficulty in understanding, and they will use this information in a diagnostic way by devoting more time to the teaching of that particular topic. But it is only infrequently that we take cognisance of perhaps the most sophisticated diagnostic information available in the classroom — the pupils own perception of whether he has attained the skill or mastered the topic in hand.

NAME: _____

Write down your honest opinion about yourself under the headings
which follow, in relation to the first half of term.

Progress

A In writing English

B In speaking and listening

C In reading and understanding literature

Difficulties: Mention any you have come across

Effort: How much have you made?

Interest and enjoyment of the course

Suggestions for changing or improving the course

Teacher's comments

Figure 3.8   Self-assessment in English

Amongst other advantages, involving pupils in assessment provides
one of the best ways of familiarising pupils with the objectives of a
course since it requires them to use the teacher's criteria in the same
way as she herself would. Thus, for example, in Figure 3.8 pupils are
asked to write comments on a 'self-assessment' form, divided in terms
of a whole range of teaching objectives, not simply cognitive attainment. The more discursive the assessment, the more individualised and
revealing it is likely to be. Grades, on the other hand, require a pupil
to think more specifically about his standard in relation to some

absolute he is striving towards, or in relation to other pupils. It is clear, however, that the way in which a teacher chooses to involve pupils in assessment will depend on its main purpose, and, in particular, whether it is for diagnosis or reporting.

Another example which is given by Ashby and Williams,[10] this time in a primary school, underlines the fact that pupil self-assessment can provide valuable information on both the affective and the cognitive components of learning. They suggest that

First of all a piece of topic writing has to be selected — preferably from a volunteer because there may well be many children who do not want their work assessed in this way. (A single piece of writing can be used with different groups.) Three is about the right size for a group, the members being sufficiently friendly for them to have confidence in voicing their own opinions. They do not need to be of the same ability. The assessment is made in two parts, first individually, and then a group discussion. When each group member has marked the writing out of ten on his own in relation to each of nine aspects — information, expression, clarity, punctuation, spelling, layout, handwriting, neatness, drawing and overall impression — the group must reach a consensus 'group mark'. During this process the group members will be forced to think carefully about the reasons for their individual marking, and this is the learning experience involved. Because the final mark sheet given to the writer is a consensus, there is little risk of personal antagonism.

Now in this approach the pupil must offer reasons for his assessment to his peers and so cannot offer a superficial or biased assessment. Of equal importance, he is learning a number of important social skills in the process. Furthermore, the approach should help pupils to understand more clearly the goals they are working towards, and at the same time give evidence of their confidence, their willingness and ability to work with others, their honesty, their readiness to accept responsibility, and so on. In the same way, if pupils are encouraged to get into the habit of evaluating something like their preparation of a particular topic for themselves, this is likely to be directly productive in fostering the skills involved such as the selection of relevant material, resourcefulness or perseverance. Initially the teacher will need to provide some kind of questionnaire or checklist to accustom the pupil to such an approach, but as he becomes more familiar with it, there are significant advantages in not structuring pupils' evaluations, since in so doing pupils will be encouraged to take more responsibility for their own learning.

Both pupils' and teachers' reactions to pupil self-assessment are interesting. For example, amongst other comments, Broadfoot[11] noted:

'I think this self assessment is a good idea because people are finding out what you like, and it makes you know truly what you feel about it.' (First year pupil)

'The teacher can see how your mind works and so in turn help you. . . . The teacher is wasting his time with the pupil who has no interest . . .'

And the teacher:

'Assuming the pupils answer honestly, a great deal about the pupil's response to the subject which would otherwise have remained hidden will be revealed. The individual child will be able to indicate clearly his own particular areas of difficulty . . .'

But, of course, the extent to which pupil self-assessment will really have an impact, is likely to depend on how it is used — if the filling in of the report is the occasion for a helpful democratic dialogue between teacher and pupil. It is easy to imagine, however, that faced with the need to allocate a grade in relation to the teacher's criteria and the need to justify that grade, the exercise will seem only an extension of existing procedures. If such a report comes at the end of a course and gives the pupil no opportunity to communicate to the teacher his essentially individual perspective — his own aims, his own problems, his own views, it is not really a self-assessment, nor is it a diagnostic assessment. Rather, such a record would need to be a much more discursive open record whose regular appearance in the classroom was an integral part of the teaching/learning process.

Figure 3.9 shows an example taken from Bosworth College, Leicester, where pupil self-assessment, as in a number of other schools, forms part of the report to parents (see chapter 5). The teachers at Bosworth feel that this mutual, written, essentially diagnostic statement helps pupils and teachers to gain trust and confidence in each other and keeps both alert to the learning process. Since specific suggestions for remedial action are required from both teacher and pupil, assessment and recording cannot be merely a collection of labelling marks and 'plastic' phrases.

So, involving pupils in an assessment dialogue is a simple means of providing a wealth of insight into the impact of teaching, how an individual pupil is coping with that teaching and its effect upon him. In particular, it can elicit information which must otherwise remain the

Bosworth College   Internal Report

Name	Date of birth	Div&T.G.	Subject &course
Joan Johnson	1.1.1967	3C	Religious knowledge

Student's Self Assessment   Date

I don't think my work has got any better since my last report. This is really because most of the written work I do is the writing up of a discussion for homework and I never really concentrate on the homework. I often become very bored in the lessons because I think the discussions last too long and after a while of listening I tend to only half pay attention, then by the time I have got round to do the homework I can vaguely remember how to do it. I think it would be a good idea if we studied the different religions of different countries. I think this would be a bit more interesting than just working from the Bible all the time

Bosworth College   Parents' Copy   Staff Assessment

Name	Date of birth	Div&T.G.	Subject &course

Staff Name   Date

Examination prospects on present performance

	O	CSE	A	CEE
strong	strong	(strong)	strong	strong
average	(average)	average	average	average
weak	weak	weak	weak	weak
ungraded	ungraded	ungraded	likely fail	

Figure 3.9   Bosworth College Internal Report

61

exclusive property of the pupil, but which may be of vital importance to the teacher in relating to that pupil. Because self-assessment is by definition voluntary — pupils cannot be forced to share their thoughts — it avoids the very serious reservations many people have about any formal assessment of 'affective' attributes whilst being extremely revealing. It is simple to operate, takes very little time or organisation and is readily incorporated into teaching. The only problem with instituting such a dialogue is likely to be its sheer novelty. Perhaps most important is the fact that involving pupils in assessment acknowledges their status as unique, independent human beings when, as so often, we are tempted to think of them merely as varieties of classroom 'fodder' — 'that girl in 3C', 'a real thicko', 'disturbed', 'John Smith up to his tricks again', 'the class joker'. Any way that helps us to penetrate behind the unquestioned stereotype to the complex, human person behind and which overtly recognises the independent status of pupils, must be a powerful ally in the educational process.

Keeping track of courses

So far in this chapter we have been principally concerned with diagnostic assessment and self-assessment as it concerns the progress of an individual pupil. Diagnostic assessment can, nevertheless, be just as important in providing feedback to the teacher on the progress of the class as a whole, and hence the success of her teaching. Concern for this kind of feedback is likely to be particularly acute when a teacher is trying out new curriculum materials, or a new pedagogic approach. Most of the hectic curriculum development activity of the 1960s and early 1970s took place outside the school, the specialist 'developers' being matched by an equally large number of specialist evaluators, supported by university and government departments or research institutes, who, in their turn, supported a large literature of books and articles. Recently, however, two major changes have been taking place. One of these changes has been a growing dissatisfaction with relying solely on the traditional 'pre-test/post-test' essentially cognitive approach to evaluating the effect of an innovation where comparison with an 'untreated' control group, supposedly identifies the specific effects of the new practice. Not only were such evaluation strategies found to be somewhat unreliable since it was almost impossible to control for all the potentially relevant variables, but they also could give almost no explanation for the effects they monitored. The forest of sophisticated evaluation strategies[12] that have replaced them are almost without exception qualitative rather than quantitative in their emphasis. At the same time there has been a growing recognition of the need to work alongside teachers if full understanding is to be achieved. It is increasingly the case too that a climate of extreme economic stringency in education means that little if any financial support will be available for development activity from outside the school, and thus that any activity of this sort will increasingly come to depend on the initiative of the individual classroom teacher.

For most teachers most of the time evaluation of their teaching will certainly be very *ad hoc* and impressionistic, and probably for most of the time not explicit. Where 'evaluation' is exclusively for the teacher's own use, the information made available by criterion-referenced tests applied before and after teaching can be an invaluable contribution to substantiating or questioning the day-to-day hunches and hypotheses which the teacher generates for herself when teaching a particular piece of curriculum. However, if a more formal evaluation is required, either for public scrutiny or if it is to be used by other parties who have not been involved in the particular classroom being considered, gauging pupils' responses is likely to be particularly difficult since none of the usual classroom assessment techniques are concerned with this. Although formal evaluation is logistically difficult for the unaided teacher, for some teachers the solution might be discussion with small groups of pupils about a particular unit of work. Other teachers may prefer to record their impressions from observing the class at work. Another approach, and one that is probably both the simplest for a teacher to operate and the most revealing, is to ask pupils directly for their comments.

A teacher's first reaction to this last suggestion is likely to be apprehension — an apprehension arising from fear of criticisms, fear that negative comments might get back to the school hierarchy and influence her promotion prospects. Thus, in this country, such evaluation has not typically been widespread and has tended to be confined to brave volunteers who have agreed to submit themselves to this as part of a research project.[13]

Interestingly enough, in the United States it is quite a different story for, especially at university level, students' evaluations are made public and provide the major basis on which subsequent students choose their courses. With this rather daunting idea in mind, any suggestion of involving pupils in the assessment process is typically greeted by a furore of teachers' union opposition. In an article in the *Times Educational Supplement*,[14] Nicholas Tucker quotes an official of the National Union of Teachers: 'It is a simple fact that children and young people are not in a position to pass judgements on their teachers, because they lack the necessary knowledge, understanding, experience and maturity .... Children are well-known to be the worst judges of their own best interests.' And another teacher union is quoted as saying it would be 'a bad job if we have to go down to the customers'.[15] Yet any teacher who has tried this will admit to being pleasantly surprised at how constructive and sensible pupils' comments are. Indeed, it has been known for a long time from research evidence that pupils' ratings of their teachers' skills agree closely with those of experts like college supervisors.[16] There are three different sorts of information a teacher can gain in this way. The first is information on curriculum content and pedagogy such as 'I like it when we do poetry but comprehension is boring' or 'I get tired of listening, I wish we could have more discussions.' Second, a teacher can get a more personal perspective on what an individual pupil is feeling — unable to keep up or held back, isolated or enjoying a group, motivated or uninterested. Third, perhaps unintentionally such feedback can provide unique insight into classroom dynamics — relationships between children that might otherwise remain private and hidden but which are very helpful for a teacher to know about in deciding how to relate to individual pupils, allocating tasks or taking remedial action.

Thus Tucker's study found the kind of feedback that pupils gave ranged from 'almost all pupils spoke negatively about their French lessons ... my form ... which was a remedial one ... simply found her lessons too hard and remote', to 'Lesley-Jane says I do big ticks which spoil her work — I thought that the big tick was a symbol of how pleased I was with it', or 'I have noticed a marked increase in socially responsible behaviour following an exercise of this [pupil assessment] kind.'

There is no space here to look in depth at the vast range of evaluation procedures which have been developed to investigate what is going on in the classroom. Suffice it to say that many of these can be adapted or adopted for use by the teacher in his classroom to look more objectively at existing practice or innovation. An awareness of some of these approaches can equip the teacher to keep track of the advantages and disadvantages of new pieces of curriculum or new teaching styles at a level which is a step above the hunch or the subjective impression which so often dictates major decisions to change or not to change, although it has to be recognised that in most cases time and resources will only allow small-scale investigations to take place.

Conclusions

This chapter has sketched out some of the ways in which assessment can make a major contribution to the improvement of pupil learning.

Examples have been given of current practice in schools where assessment is not seen essentially as fodder for markbooks or school reports. Little mention has been made of the notion of 'continuous assessment' because in so many cases application of the idea in schools has reduced it to nothing more than a staccato form of terminal assessment which places a still greater assessment burden on pupils without giving them any more opportunity to learn from their mistakes.

It is disturbing that in most books on assessment and assessment techniques which have been published in Britain over the last twenty years or so, crucial areas such as assessment for diagnosis, pupil self-assessment and teacher-based evaluation techniques[17] have received scant attention. This is perhaps not surprising, however, when one looks at the millions of pounds which are spent each year on external examinations and their infrastructure, and the overwhelming demands which society's perception of the importance of certification places on the teacher. It is manifestly less easy to show that well thought out programmes of diagnostic assessment and remedial action are improving pupil attainment and radically altering their motivation and perception of the value of education than it is to point to a 3 per cent increase in the number of pupils who have attained an external certificate and make the appropriate boast at speech day. It is much more impressive to state on you job application for an assistant head teacher post that you have been a marker with the London GCE Board for three years than to state that you have consistently and conscientiously diagnosed pupil difficulties on core learning objectives. If you have entered teaching because of your interest in physics rather than your interest in children, it is perhaps more rewarding to create a new set of worksheets than to develop a set of tests. But the overwhelming evidence is that to use diagnostic procedures over a period of time is likely to increase pupil attainment, develop motivation and consequently change pupil attitudes to school.

But, of course, there are problems. The design of good criterion-referenced tests, self-evaluation schedules and evaluation strategies is difficult and it is also time-consuming. However, we have suggested in this book that resources are gradually becoming available, and it is up to the individual teacher to use them. Perhaps more important is that individual teachers recognise that where they are not able to provide adequate resources on their own, they should co-operate with other interested colleagues in creating tests and instruments on a collaborative basis. Equally, it has to be recognised that school assessment systems which retain the unnecessary relics of Old Normgrade do not lend themselves to supporting these approaches. The onus must, therefore, be on head teachers to question the assumptions which they have about their school assessment programme, and if they are even partly convinced of the importance of assessment as an aid to learning, allow and encourage interested teachers by giving them the opportunity to develop alternatives to the traditional model.

Chapter 4

'The ghost in the machine':
keeping track of personal progress

Wester Hailes Community Education Centre is a large modern community school in a sprawling suburban housing development. Many of the classes, as well as being open to pupils, are open to adults of all ages and backgrounds.

During the intensive planning period which preceded the school's first intake of pupils, the school worked hard in developing a co-ordinated policy on curriculum, pedagogy and assessment which it thought to be essential. As far as assessment was concerned, it was strongly felt by many of the staff that the traditional 'class test' approach would be very threatening to participating adults and would be counter-productive to learning in encouraging the insecurity that so often characterises mature students. What was needed was a more co-operative approach to assessment which would be suitable for both younger and older students. In particular, Wester Hailes wanted an approach which would reflect the fact that, as a community school, its aims were broader than a normal school, especially in relation to the personal and social development of the members of its community. In the event, different departments developed their own procedures in relation to their own particular goals in which common themes were evident — profile assessment, collaborative assessment, the inclusion of personal qualities, and, where appropriate, an emphasis on mastery rather than grading. General school policy was that records should reflect a detailed breakdown of progress in a subject in relation to its various activities and skills. Equally the records were to be as far as possible the product of both teacher and student evaluation of every aspect of learning in relation to some pre-defined standard.

Figure 4.1 shows the assessment profile sheet for a second-year module of a home economics course in the school. At the beginning of the course each student was given a specification of the intended

HOME ECONOMICS DEPARTMENT

DATE: STUDENT:

FOOD MODULE II   TEACHER: GROUP LEADER: CLASS:

AIMS of MODULE: to apply knowledge of nutrition gained in Module I to the planning and preparation of family meals

CHECKLIST OF OBJECTIVES	USUALLY		SOMETIMES		RARELY		TEACHER'S COMMENT:
TEACHER/STUDENT ASSESS.	T	S	T	S	T	S	
SKILLS:							
Follows instructions well							
Uses/cares for equip. well							
Plans/organises work well							
Uses tools skilfully							
Observes clearly							
Solves problems well							
ATTITUDE/EFFORT/CO-OP.							STUDENT'S COMMENT:
Listens attentively							
Works willingly							
Works well with others							
Works to ability							

Completed module to teacher's satisfaction   YES   NO

UNDERSTANDING/RECALL OF KNOWLEDGE	TEST SCORE	RECOMMENDATION FOR S3	TEACHER	STUDENT
Excellent understanding/recall		Skills: Catering/H-making		
Good " " / "		Possible 'O' Grade		
Average " " / "		Definite 'O' Grade		
Poor " " / "		Not recommended		
Unsatisfactory " / "				

Figure 4.1   The assessment profile for a second-year home economics course at Wester Hailes Community

learning outcomes, and so the aim of the module, 'To apply knowledge of nutrition gained in module 1 to the planning and preparation of family meals', is only an outline reminder for the users of the assessment profile.

Analysis of the profile shows that it includes twenty-seven separate pieces of information, fifteen of which are supplied by the teacher, and twelve by the student. The three extra categories supplied by the teacher are the test score, evaluation of the student's ability to understand and recall knowledge, and a simple statement as to whether the student had completed the module to the teacher's satisfaction. For the ten categories under the 'skills' and 'attitude/effort/co-operation' headings, both the teacher and the student have to decide, for example, whether the student 'solves problems well' 'usually', 'sometimes' or 'rarely'. Both student and teacher have to provide a summative account on the work of the student during the course and both have to make a prognostic recommendation for courses in the third year.

Wester Hailes' approach to assessment echoes a number of the points made earlier in this book in our discussion of diagnostic assessment. Although this chapter is to focus particularly on the assessment of those attributes sometimes termed 'work-related' or 'non-cognitive', or more formally 'the affective domain', it is already clear from looking at the home economics record that when we discuss real school situations, we cannot divide the personal from the academic in assessment any more than we can in teaching. And yet Wester Hailes is not typical in its approach, and herein is the justification for a chapter explicitly on 'non-cognitive' assessment. Most schools are loath to include any open formal recording of such attributes in their records because of the profound suspicion that exists of any 'big brother' monitoring of this kind. On the other hand, at an informal level, non-cognitive assessment pervades every aspect of school functioning. Thus, the question is, should it be made explicit?

Some reasons for non-cognitive assessment

With a little thought it should be apparent that the reason for making assessments of non-cognitive characteristics are the same as they are for making assessment of 'academic' progress. The first is its potential contribution to the evaluation of courses which have been a 'hit' or a 'miss'. Second, is its potential value for providing information on summative 'attainment' or information which may be of predictive value and can therefore be of help in guiding pupils. The third role of such assessment, and probably the most important, and at the same time most frequently overlooked, is its potential for diagnosing problems which pupils are having with the development of non-cognitive characteristics, and, consequently, offering potential for the reinforcement of such qualities. It may well be that where an aspect such as motivation is explicitly recognised through assessment as a key factor in learning, this can provide a channel of communication through which motivation can actually be improved.

However, not least because the assessment of non-cognitive objectives and the explicit notion of teaching for them is considered by many teachers to be innovatory, if not contentious, it is worth looking beyond this rather shallow veneer in search of more systematic arguments as to why it might be important to make such assessments.

To begin with, it has become increasingly common for schools, subject departments, individual teachers, curriculum packages, and reports of expert committees to state categorically that the development of affective pupil characteristics, such as, for example, attitudes to work, relationship with peers and self-concept, is, or should be, part of a school's responsibility. Almost by definition, therefore, it becomes the responsibility of the teacher to develop these characteristics unless he is willing to stand up and argue a case why he should not. It follows, therefore, that if a systematic attempt is to be made to teach towards such objectives, so it becomes incumbent upon the teacher to find out whether or not he is succeeding in the same way that he will evaluate pupil progress in relation to academic goals. Needless to say, this is not a position which is held by all educationists, but the reality of the situation is that the vast majority of those teachers who agree with it in principle rarely put it into practice except when required to write confidential reports or testimonials.

Less controversial, but no less important, is that, as we have pointed out in chapter 3, pupils' affective characteristics such as interest, attitude, and self-perception when studying a particular piece of work can have a considerable impact on cognitive attainment. Bloom, for example, has estimated that up to 25 per cent of the variation in school achievement can be accounted for by such affective characteristics.[1] Thus, not only can the development of affective pupil characteristics be seen to be important in its own right, but their development is clearly a vital contributing factor to learning in its broader context. Consequently, just as it is a sound argument that teachers should assess pupil attainment of important, cognitive, core-intended outcomes with a view to taking remedial action, or, where appropriate, to use such information in a predictive context or for course evaluation, so the same arguments again apply to the assessment of important affective intended outcomes.

Another sound reason for developing systematic and reliable affective assessment techniques, is that there is considerable evidence that teachers take such factors into account anyway. Thus, for example, research by Greany and Kellaghan found that non-cognitive assessment can account for at least 50 per cent of the basis for class placement and even more among pupils with low cognitive achievement.[2] In another study[3] of the basis on which teachers are likely to differentiate between pupils, it was found that the six key characteristics were:

The involvement of the pupil in the learning situation;
The ability the pupil has in the subject;
His overall ability;
His behaviour;
The quality and tidiness of work presented, and
The interest displayed by the pupil in the subject.

A somewhat similar study of the criteria for secondary school selection[4] found that 55 per cent of teachers took attitude into consideration, and 33 per cent of these also included aspects such as honesty, obedience, sincerity, politeness, truthfulness, etc. And yet unless their attention is specifically directed towards a conscious consideration of these other attributes, teachers tend to discuss pupils almost exclusively in terms of a category which might be called 'general ability'.[5] It is very rare indeed for a teacher to seek to assess such qualities in any overt systematic way.[6] It seems likely, therefore, that most teachers would agree that although[7]

we make no formal attempt to assess non-cognitive qualities. . . . All the points are inherent in the assessment because it is so subjective. You cannot assess a child whom you have taught for five terms, and not have in your assessment some recognition of these qualities. It's impossible.

Related to this is a further substantial point that there is a good deal of evidence that teachers would like to see more formal recording of non-cognitive attributes. In a Scottish study,[8] more than 50 per cent of teachers felt a profile record should include some rating of interest, perseverance, reliability, effort, acceptance of discipline, carefulness, enterprise, co-operation, responsibility, attendance, punctuality, confidence and self-reliance. Nevertheless, the same study found that only half of a sample of thirty-two secondary schools included any information on pupils' progress which was not specifically subject-oriented, and, even then, this was typically limited to 'effort' or 'behaviour' on a 'good' or 'poor' basis. Indeed, recent attempts by the DES Assessment of Performance Unit to monitor aspects of pupils' personal development on a national basis, evoked a storm of protest and has had to be abandoned at least for the foreseeable future.[9]

Thus, we seem to be dealing here with a profound paradox. On the one hand, teachers typically set a great deal of store by non-cognitive objectives in their teaching,[10] and many of them would like to include progress in relation to such objectives in their records. Most teachers recognise that the non-cognitive characteristics of pupils significantly affect the various judgments they are required to make. Equally, most teachers spend a good deal of time writing references and testimonials which include a good deal of their subjective impressions about a pupil's character and behaviour. Yet very few indeed make any *formal* attempt to collect such information systematically, and resist vociferously any outside attempt to impose such tests. Indeed, it may fairly be said that:[11]

> at the moment we have the disquieting situation in which teachers make their judgments like amateurs in the field of those objectives which are often regarded as the most important; and are subject to all those prejudices, stereotypes, distortions, etc. to which all people are exposed when they have only their common sense to rely on.

Why not non-cognitive?

Despite these apparently overwhelming arguments for the sound and systematic development and assessment of non-cognitive characteristics, it is clear from some of the paradoxes we have noted above that such assessment is rarely taken seriously.

Why teachers are so wary of formalising this kind of assessment is to some extent an historical question. After the horrors of the 'gentling the masses' programme inherent in the 'payment by results' system[12] of the mid-nineteenth century, teachers have been reluctant to recognise any basis for distinction between pupils other than academic merit. It was not realised that non-cognitive characteristics of various kinds were inevitably a profound influence on all such assessments, and little attention was thus given to developing tests in this area as the educational testing movement burgeoned. As a result, a vicious circle has developed that teachers are reluctant to intrude their assessing activities still further into pupils' lives, particularly in view of the fact that few techniques exist to help them cut down the amount of subjectivity involved. Yet they recognise that such characteristics do influence pupils' progress to a considerable extent and ought somehow to be taken note of. Mostly the solution is the provision of a written statement, since because this is clearly subjective, it is apparent for what it is, and makes no formal claim to be more than an opinion. But is this really the best way to make such observations? How biased are such comments? How comparable are the standards used between different teachers and schools? What ultimately are such reports for? As usual, it is this last question that must be answered before we can give any detailed consideration to available techniques.

Their reluctance is also attributable to the lack of value consensus in our multi-cultural society, and teachers' consequent hesitation to impose their own values and norms of behaviour on their pupils. This problem is a deeply personal one well beyond the scope of this book. The complexity of the issue is, however, manifested by evidence such as that from another Scottish study[13] that 44 per cent of the teachers who were asked if affective pupil characteristics should be included on a certificate issued by schools were in favour, 44 per cent were against and the remainder undecided.

Our position here will simply be that if you decide to pass comment in respect of this kind of attribute, you may wish to avail yourselves of some of the approaches of this book in order to do it more reliably. And secondly, if we fight shy of admitting we assess such attributes, we ought equally to fight shy of including them as teaching intentions, or of reporting them on such things as UCCA forms and in personal references. On the other hand, if we are certain that we can and should foster qualities like responsibility, co-operation, enterprise and confidence in our teaching, we must recognise that our educational tradition is such that our efforts are correspondingly undermined to the extent that their outcomes are not assessed. In particular, there is strong argument that where the teaching objectives of a subject are predominantly in the affective domain, that is to say, non-cognitive, the necessity for non-traditional affective assessment is correspondingly increased.

What might we assess?

Before we turn to some thinking on, and examples of, how non-cognitive assessment might be made, it is worth considering briefly what might be assessed. In general terms we have already seen that the 'affective domain' differentiated from the cognitive and psychomotor domains comprises attitudes, feelings, values, emotions, interests, and so on. For simplicity, in this book, we will consider two broad sub-divisions of this domain as it relates to school work: pupil attitudes, and pupil personal characteristics.

Pupil attitude, which embraces variables such as interest, enjoyment, values, etc., is clearly related to cognitive concerns. Thus, a teacher may find it useful to evaluate a new course by considering the extent to which it has held the interest of the class. She may also consider the extent to which it has contributed to their valuing certain attitudinal objectives such as feeling that physics has an important part to play in modern society, or that modern sculpture is an interesting and varied art form. When we turn to pupil personal characteristics, such as a pupil's ability to work in a team situation, or to develop skills of leadership, affective variables become less related to the content of a particular subject and might be considered rather as intended learning outcomes in their own right. Clearly, though, they do not exist in a vacuum, and indeed, they vary from classroom to classroom. An outstanding common feature of both broad categories, however, is that they comprise a large number of different affective qualities.

How, then, might a teacher come to decide on which non-cognitive variables she should stress in her teaching and hence her assessment? There would seem to be three ways of entering the maze and we will look at each of them in turn.

1 Common sense

Whilst we have for a long time been aware of the vagaries of cognitive assessment — problems of whether the assessments of different raters of tests are comparable (reliability) or whether we are in fact measuring what we think we are measuring (validity), these spectres seem not to disturb many current attempts in schools to make more subjective non-cognitive judgment. And yet they should, for there is evidence to suggest that what teachers say should be assessed, and the constructs they actually use in making assessments, are different. Thus it cannot be assumed that if a reference or report form requires comment on 'conscientiousness' all teachers will interpret this characteristic according to the same range of behaviours. In one study,[14] for example, six teachers in a department were asked to list the non-cognitive characteristics which they would like to assess. This resulted in twenty-one characteristics being put forward, which the teachers hypothesised could be reduced into five groups. However, when they were asked to assess their pupils on these twenty-one variables, the results suggested that how they *thought* the characteristics grouped together was only in part a true reflection of the way they actually *used* them. For example, although the notion of 'general class behaviour' had eight characteristics in their hypothesised grouping, there was only a very weak relationship between these characteristics in the assessments made. In short, the idea of choosing what should be assessed on the basis of unsystematic guess work, has many potential pitfalls.

2 Using existing testing priorities

Anyone who has done a little reading in the fields of educational psychology or educational testing will be aware that there are a number of existing tests for non-cognitive characteristics. Amongst these might be included measurements of anxiety of which one reviewer[15] noted approximately 3,500 articles or books in the period 1950-63 alone. Achievement-motivation, attitude, self-concept, socio-metric status, introversion, extroversion and many others have all equally received a good deal of attention. The basic problems with nearly all of these tests are first that they are by and large designed to be applied and interpreted by trained educational psychologists; second, they are essentially instruments for research or specialist application; and, third, even where their focus may be of interest to classroom teachers, their construction typically requires considerable expertise and resources which are not available in most schools. In short, therefore, both the focus and the nature of existing testing practices makes them unsuitable for the majority of day-to-day teaching situations.

3 Evidence on teachers' implicit perceptions of non-cognitive variables

There is considerable, and surprisingly consistent evidence on the number, and indeed the nature, of non-cognitive characteristics which teachers tend to take into account when considering their pupils. Previous work based on factor analysis suggests that when making assessments of a number of non-cognitive characteristics, most of the teachers' perceptions of differences amongst pupils can typically be explained by two to five factors. In one study, for example,[16] Hope concluded that teachers basically saw pupils in terms of the characteristics which allocated them to the categories 'even tempered plodder' and 'pushful innovator'. Other studies have found as the key characteristics 'satisfactory classroom behaviour' and 'group leadership',[17] 'classroom behaviour' and 'social behaviour',[18] while work on the Continent has come forward with very similar results.[19] Consequently, if a decision on what is to be assessed is to be based on existing evidence as to what teachers typically take into account in making non-cognitive assessments of pupils, there is considerable existing work on the subject. As we will argue below, however, what typically happens may not be the best basis from which to proceed.

It is clear that a non-cognitive assessment policy based solely on common sense, existing testing priorities, or teachers' implicit perceptions, is unlikely to result in a satisfactory outcome. 'Common sense' can easily result in making assessments which combine several affective characteristics which objective inspection may reveal as independent. A choice based on what teachers perceive to be distinct may result in turn in assessing variables which common sense indicates to be inappropriate to a given situation. Introducing existing tests or test procedures may well further confuse the teacher's original desire for information. As we will argue below, the only solution is to develop a clear, systematic and professional approach to making decisions on both affective assessment and the affective component of our curricula. The alternative is to risk the danger of perpetuating the existing situation in which, almost inevitably, many teachers' assessments of non-cognitive characteristics are subject to errors that 'are so serious that statements about pupils reveal more about the attitudes of the rater than they do about the pupil'.[20]

Making non-cognitive assessments

In the rest of this book we have not concentrated on the techniques which might be used to make assessments. Where non-cognitive assessments are concerned, however, the fact that traditional textbook designs are often inappropriate, suggests that the teacher who decides to keep track of such intended outcomes may well welcome the inclusion of some observations on such techniques in this chapter. Basically there are two ways in which non-cognitive assessments can be made: inquiry systems and observational systems. Both of these approaches have certain advantages, but, as we will see below, neither of them provides an 'off the shelf' solution for the classroom teacher.

Inquiry systems

Inquiry systems of non-cognitive assessment involve posing questions which are designed to give information to the teacher on an individual's or a group's 'score' in relation to a given non-cognitive characteristic. Popham[21] sub-divides such systems into 'low inference' approaches where individuals are given questions, statements or verbal stimuli, and the response to these 'if truthful can be readily interpreted without making any major inferential leaps' and 'high inference' approaches in which the tester has to 'make a pretty healthy inferential jump to interpret the data as reflective of an individual's affective dispositions'.

Low inference inquiry systems have been used widely by psychologists, and by and large, their's has been almost the only source of development work in the realm of non-cognitive assessment. Their techniques such as projective tests, semantic differential or repertory-grid scales, sound, and often are, highly technical. There have been attempts to adapt some of these essentially research techniques for normal classroom use. Raven, for example, has sought to adopt for classroom use, a technique pioneered by McClelland[22] of analysing a subject's interpretation of a series of pictures. But even if a teacher were to be provided with such a test, it is unlikely that she would be either willing or able to allocate the time necessary for an individual interview with each pupil. Semantic differential and repertory-grid techniques require the respondent to register a level of agreement or disagreement with a range of statements. These might lend themselves to class assessment more readily if designed to be administered in the same way as the usual kind of class tests. It is, however, unlikely that tests would be commercially available that matched the precise range of attributes any particular teacher or department felt was relevant to assess in relation to their teaching. Yet without such a match, the tests would not be particularly helpful in 'keeping track of teaching' and would thus not fulfil the kind of assessment role set out in this book. Nor is it likely that teachers would be in a position to design their own tests, lacking both the requisite time and knowledge.

Attitude scales, of which those of Thurstone, Guttman and Lickert are amongst the most well known, are also techniques which have now reached a high level of sophistication but which do not lend themselves to amateur development and use in the classroom. Although such scales have been widely used by students as the basis for small classroom studies, they can be very misleading unless carefuly constructed and tested. At any event they are unlikely to provide particularly useful records of individual progress.

We are left with interviews and various kinds of observations. The value of interviews is fairly self-evident, and can be great if skilfully conducted. In reality, however, it is unlikely that many teachers can contemplate finding the time to sit down for thirty minutes or so with each individual pupil to discuss his feelings about his progress even if she could convince herself that the pupil would not find this situation so threatening as to render it virtually valueless.

77

The overwhelming problem with each of these low inference systems, however, is that they each more or less equate with asking a pupil 'Are you a good leader', 'Do you value drama as part of your curriculum?' and so on. With the proviso that it is possible to minimise misleading responses by a variety of techniques, such as submerging crucial questions amongst a group of trivial or non-controversial questions, it has to be recognised that such devices are open to faking if for any reason the respondent sees fit to do so.

One way of reducing the risk of faking is to use high inference assessment systems for the simple reason that as Popham[23] suggests: 'Just as they require an inference on the part of the evaluator, they also require a comfortable inference from the individual responding to the measure'. Thus a teacher may decide to set an essay on 'the siting of a nuclear power station' where the overt reason may be to assess the pupils' knowledge of the factors affecting such a locational choice, while the covert intention is to evaluate the degree to which pupils have come to value the outlook of the 'environmentalist' lobby, or to take the opposing viewpoint. Clearly, there is little scope in such high inference techniques for individual assessment, but the data provided could be invaluable in curricular evaluation where it is focused on the overall response.

An interesting practical example of such an approach can be seen at Shakespeare School, a new, suburban, academically orientated comprehensive where there is a good deal of overt endorsement of the need for the school to provide for personal development. One manifestation of this concern is the provision in the school of a fully equipped theatre. Yet at Shakespeare School the drama teachers have encountered considerable difficulty with discipline and motivation. This may be partly because drama cannot be conducted in a formal way and pupils use the period to "let off steam". Partly it is because, despite the school's theoretical commitment to a broadly based curriculum, the strong academic orientation discourages pupils from seeing drama as important. The teachers have sought to counteract this problem by setting pupils to think and to write about how and why they learn drama, for the teacher and for each other, and this in turn offers considerable insight at a curriculum evaluation level. The ambiguity is well expressed by the following extract (original spelling):

Jane: 'What is drama at school for?'
Anne: 'Well Jane it is for getting on with other people, working well in a group and learning about other people, and also it is for letting yourself express in various ways your feelings'.
Jane: 'Wouldn't you rather go to another lesson instead of coming

to drama?'

Me: 'No, not realy, it is a good break from other lessons and it makes your imagination work more than in other lessons.'

Jane: 'What was it like at first?'

Me: 'At first it was good but now we get more interesting things so it is a little better, the trouble is know one wants to co-operate.'

Jane: 'Do you still enjoy drama?'

Me: 'Yes, but it's a bit boaring, you don't get much acting by yourself, you eather get none or some with a group.'

In general, pupils at Shakespeare are well aware of the potential value of drama for their self-development — for developing greater awareness of the world and of themselves; for enhancing concentration, imagination, self-control, co-operation, confidence, speech, self-expression, physical fitness and relaxation, aesthetic responsiveness, and even for developing the communication skills important in getting a job. To some extent, the low level of commitment to this subject may be attributed to adolescent self-consciousness, but mostly it is clear that pupils feel that subjects not culminating in qualifications, however desirable educationally, are a waste of time. The outcome of this high inference inquiry system of attitudinal assessment clearly highlighted these points and thus provides more objective data on which to base the direction of further developments.

The overwhelming problem with each of these inquiry systems, however, is that existing developments have not been designed for use in the classroom by teachers wanting to keep track of their own teaching. There is considerable scope for more systematic classroom-oriented work in the future, but at the present time it has to be recognised that most of the non-cognitive assessment which takes place in schools is based on teacher observation of pupils.

Observational systems

Few people with any familiarity with schools at all would dispute that teachers' observations of pupils' non-cognitive characteristics is one of the most basic currencies of school conversation. 'Comments' sections on school reports are the archetypal repositories of 'tries hard' (effort) and 'could do better' (application); the air in parent/teacher meetings is thick with affective innuendo; staffroom tongues wag with the tale of the head's son's apathy, belligerence or docility. In short, teachers constantly make informal assessments of pupils' non-cognitive characteristics based on their observation of overt pupil behaviour.

But as we have already hinted, there are problems with such informal and unsystematic techniques. Characteristics may not be clearly defined, leading to problems of ambiguity, validity and relevance. These are the general problems. But most fundamental is that no one, including teachers, can observe feelings; they can only observe actions which presumably reflect these feelings, and, in making such inferences, they may be wrong. Certainly, the discrepancy already discussed between pupils' and teachers' estimates in this respect is indicative. Secondly, teachers may simply not have enough time or opportunity to observe particular behaviour sufficiently to get an accurate and properly weighted picture.

Of course, the inadequacy of 'effort' or 'attitude' graded on a one to five normal distribution as the sole manifestation of non-cognitive assessment has long been recognised, and many teachers in schools have attempted to make their observational systems meaningful, and, at the same time, more objective. Thus, for example, in the technical education department of Wester Hailes Community Education Centre, the teachers have adopted an approach in which various criteria have been agreed on as guides to awarding a grade at a particular level (Table 4.1). This is a procedure which will be familiar to many teachers as it is widely used and is relatively simple to do. But there are several disadvantages with this kind of approach. First, the statements are in many cases ambiguous and open to a great deal of variation in their interpretation (inter-rater reliability). Second, they are comparative — each depends on the other — rather than being oriented to the more positive approach of levels of mastery. Third, we cannot be sure that what we think we are assessing — for example, effort — is truly reflected in the intuitive indices we have devised (validity). And, finally, it is not always made clear why particular categories have been singled out for comment and whether these are, in fact, the most crucial in relation to the learning of a particular subject — the basis is again an intuitive one.

An approach which relates observations more closely to actual incidents in the classroom is described in the work of one recent research project.[24] Again in a technical education department, the teachers were asked to specify incidents which they felt to be reflective of the various levels normally referred to by grades or words such as 'good' and 'fair'. Thus, for 'effort' the teachers came up with indices such as:

'A pupil who works steadily from the beginning to the end.'
'Voluntary preparation for work done at home.'
'Talks a great deal.'
'Takes short cuts.'
'Work is full of careless mistakes.'

TABLE 4.1   *Wester Hailes Education Centre Technical Education Assessment (Bank of Comments)*

These comments are intended to help standardise student's reports. Meetings will also be held at regular intervals to standardise the standard of craftsmanship in the department.

ATTITUDE

1 Keen and interested
   Works hard at all times
2 Works very steadily
   Shows some interest and enthusiasm
3 Works erratically
   Works well when interested
4 Easily satisfied with an inferior job
   Requires constant prodding
5 Apathetic
   Lazy and disinterested

UNDERSTANDING

1 Thinks logically and remembers material taught
   Will readily understand verbal instructions and explanations
2 Subject matter recently taught is remembered and used
   Has a good technical vocabulary
3 Follows explanations and thinks out simple problems
   Can normally understand and act on routine instructions
4 Subject matter taught is soon forgotten if not used constantly
   Has difficulty in understanding instructions
5 Cannot remember even recently taught work
   Does not understand even simple instructions

SKILLS

1 Works quickly and to a very fine standard
   Handles tools with a lot of confidence
2 Will use tools naturally and well after demonstration
   Produces a good standard of work
3 When shown will use tools in a controlled manner
   Produces a reasonable standard of work
4 Has difficulty in using hand tools
   Cannot work very accurately with materials
5 Looks very awkward with hand tools
   Gets movements muddled and wrong

TABLE 4.2   *A scale defining various gradations of 'effort' in a technical education department*

GOOD

1   A pupil who is prepared to work steadily from the beginning of the period to the end.

As soon as one (process job) is completed, the pupil is eager to get on with the next one.

Does not get put off by awkward or difficult problems, works them out and sees the job through to completion.

Voluntary preparation for practical work done at home, e.g. drawings, etc.

Works hard until the job is completed.

Makes attempt to continue working without further instructions.

2   Does not waste time talking.

Works steadily.

Works well in class when given a job to do.

Shows some interest and enthusiasm for the subject.

3   Works 'erratically', sometimes eager and keen, at other times lazy.

Steady worker but has more potential than he/she displays.

Expends reasonable degree of effort — sufficient to get by.

If a certain job really interests him he will work hard but if the job in hand does not appeal, very little effort is applied.

4   Interest wanes if success is slow to come.

Never exerts or pushes himself. Eventually the work is done however.

Easily satisfied with an inferior job.

5   Always reluctant to start work.

He/she requires constant prodding.

Spends too much time window gazing, could work a lot harder.

Dislikes physical effort.

BAD

6   Lazy, putting no thought or physical effort into his work.

Completely apathetic.

Very idle student.

Even when pushed, this pupil will look for excuses to stop work.

Destructive in his attitude.

Will actually destroy or 'lose' an item of work rather than attempt to complete it.

The statements included in this scale were agreed by all members of the department to be good examples of the sort of behaviour which would be associated with the point on the scale to which it was allotted. By setting an aim that everyone should achieve at least a two on the scale, the teacher is thus able to distinguish between those pupils who are applying satisfactory effort, and those who require some assistance. Later work suggested that a four point scale would perhaps have been easier to use.

Some fifteen or so such descriptions were generated by each of the seven teachers in the department, all of them referring as closely as possible to unambiguous and specific activity which is likely to provide for high inter-rater agreement. Thus 'talks a great deal' is much more unambiguous than 'rarely pays attention'. There is still a measure of vagueness, since 'a great deal' is not defined, and perhaps 'is never silent for more than two minutes' is open to more accurate assessment, but a line has to be drawn at the point between where pedantry begins to outweigh convenience.

It was found useful at the stage where the scale was being agreed by the department (Table 4.2) for several teachers to assess the same set of pupils on the basis of these criteria so that subsequently in comparing the point on the scale to which each pupil was allocated, they can see which criteria are producing a consensus and which are still vague enough to allow a significant range of personal interpretation. Pupils do, of course, behave differently with different teachers, and thus sometimes discrepancies in teachers' assessments will reflect real variation. Ideally, though, what is being sought is a set of descriptions which could be validly used by a neutral observer sitting at the back of the class.

If the teachers are to use this information for diagnostic purposes, the next step is for the teachers concerned to identify the most consistent and valid behavioural descriptors for each characteristic they have decided to assess. They then have to decide at which point on the continuum they would divide pupils into two major categories, perhaps 'satisfactory' and 'needs help'. This notion is essentially the same as setting a 'cut-off' score on a criterion-referenced multiple choice test and is, of course, to some extent arbitrary.[25]

Nevertheless, it is important to try to get away from stopping one's thinking at the deeply ingrained four- or five-point scale approach at least for classroom purposes. The 'grade on a scale approach' tends to emphasise comparison with other pupils when what is most often needed in relation to teaching is a maximum of diagnostic information in order that the teacher can seek to overcome the causes of specific problems.

The most interesting contrast between inquiry and observational systems of making non-cognitive assessments is that while the former is an approach devised outside the classroom, the latter has grown out of *existing practices*. Thus, while as we have already seen, inquiry systems *may* have future potential in helping teachers to keep track of teaching, observational systems are with us at the present time. The issue therefore, is whether the teacher who is faced with the problem of developing and assessing attitudes and personal characteristics, can recognise the inadequacies of the present system and feel that they are important enough to overcome.

Conclusions

For most teachers the justification of non-cognitive assessment will be that by noting those pupils whose attitudes or behaviour is hindering their progress and, in many cases, the reason for this, they have taken the initial step towards overcoming the problem. On the other hand, as far as using such information for reporting is concerned, the emphasis is likely to be more on building up a summative picture of the pupil as a whole. At the reporting stage too some measure of 'norm-referencing' − or comparison with other pupils − may also be present. The distinction between these two different kinds of non-cognitive assessment needs to be kept clearly in mind since the major controversy about non-cognitive assessment attaches to the problem of what information the school is justified in giving to the outside world. As far as non-cognitive assessment in relation to learning progress is concerned, we are merely concerned here with making more systematic and comparable − and hence reliable − that mass of impressionistic information which must inform the day-to-day, and even minute-to-minute, decision-making of the teacher in the classroom. This is reasonably safe ground on which to tread, but the reporting issue is much more contentious. Thus, for example, Brown,[26] while accepting that non-cognitive assessment, for all its shortcomings, can usefully be incorporated in assessment which is primarily oriented to monitoring, diagnosis and guidance, has severe reservations about it for any more formal purposes:

> Assessment of attitudes in education is at a primitive stage partly because of confusion about the meanings of terms and inadequacy of assessment instruments. But more fundamentally, the purposes of, and justifications for teaching towards attitude goals, and assessing their achievements, have not been given close enough scrutiny: and that scrutiny involves examination of the moral and rational basis of the demands that are made upon teachers or pupils in asking them to accept responsibility in the affective domain.

Nevertheless, despite Brown's reservations, the existence of UCCA forms, detailed questionnaires from prospective employers, and the constant demands on schools for character references on pupils from many sources, puts on to the teacher a demand from society which she has to meet. Truly to keep track of teaching in the affective domain therefore requires the teacher to polish her assessment instruments perhaps even harder than she does for more traditional areas of testing.

In this chapter we have specifically been concerned with keeping track of those work-related characteristics of pupils so central to teaching, learning, and, indeed, selection. We have recognised that a distinction between the cognitive and the affective is impossible in this respect because progress towards intellectual goals and the related cognitive assessments influence and are influenced by the prevailing affective kaleidoscope. Thus all we have sought to do in this chapter is to suggest a number of ways in which teachers can make more systematic and overt that mass of impressionistic information they gather about their pupils as they teach. In this way we hope teachers will on the one hand be encouraged to give increasing and explicit recognition to the importance of work-related attributes, and, by so doing, help the development of positive attributes in their pupils. On the other hand, we hope that teachers will be able to develop a more systematic and valid basis for the non-cognitive reports that they are frequently required to write.

In the course of our discussion on the troubled subject of non-cognitive recording, the distinction between assessment in and for the classroom, and assessment for other purposes has become increasingly explicit. In a book primarily concerned with the relationship between assessment and teaching, we could leave aside all those dilemmas associated with more public forms of assessment as beyond the scope of the present discussion. To do so, however, would be to fail to take cognisance of the fact that the various levels of assessment concern in the school are inevitably closely related. On the one hand, teachers are the only valid source of a whole range of valuable insights about the performance and potential of a pupil. On the other hand, the form and content of a school's reporting of its pupils' achievements, and indeed the way the school evaluates itself, will exert a powerful backwash effect on its organisational and curricular priorities at classroom level, and hence of classroom assessment policy. In recognition of this fact the following two chapters shift the emphasis from recording and diagnosing pupils' learning progress to the identification, recording and reporting of their achievement both for within school purposes, and for communication outside the school.

Chapter 5

Dealing with achievement:
reporting, monitoring and the accountability issue

As we saw in chapter 1, and as will be underlined when we look at reporting in chapter 6, the 'customers' of education include not only pupils, but parents, employers and other educational institutions. Furthermore, the providers of education comprise not only the teachers who have individual contact with the pupil, but also the immediate superiors of the individual teachers who are paid to take responsibility for an infant department, a subject department and so on. Responsibility for a child's learning is further vested in the head teacher of the school, the local education authority, and ultimately, the state.

And so, just as it is the legitimate and vital concern of the teacher to keep careful track of the progress of his pupils, so it can be argued that this progress, or lack of it, is the legitimate concern of many other interested parties. Equally, while the outcomes of assessment form the basis of a teacher's evaluation of her pupil's progress, so the assessment of achievement may form the basis of the accountability of a teacher, or of a school, or of the system as a whole to its various customers.

Needless to say this whole area of 'accountability' is riddled with tensions. To begin with, the very idea is seen by many teachers as a slight on their professional competence. This is exacerbated by their working in a system which, at least superficially, values professional autonomy in choosing what and how they should teach. The idea behind this chapter, therefore, is to explain some of the ways in which assessment of achievement and accountability come together and to look at some of the arguments and the tensions which have resulted from certain attempts to make accountability more explicit.

Accountability from within the school

Reporting in Whitehill Secondary School

The lower school complex of Whitehill Secondary School is a large and impressive structure reminiscent of a departmental store. Each subject department has an 'area', but no walls separate the intense activity of the artists from that of the mathematicians across the way. Within the school there is a constant movement between the open plan teaching area, resources centres, lecture theatres and a mass of modern amenities.

To take full advantage of such facilities, the school policy is to encourage pupils to work and learn as far as possible at their own rate. Needless to say this raises problems for the teacher, not least in keeping track of individual progress. Increasingly, it was felt that the traditional 'grading' approach to assessment was not providing teachers or pupils with the sort of information which they required to direct pupils to the most appropriate courses for their needs, and so the school moved forward to develop an alternative system.

Each department was asked to define criteria for success in their courses at three levels; core, extension 1, and extension 2. 'Core' was defined as work involving the basic skills and knowledge that all pupils should possess. 'Extension 1' comprised more demanding work for 'average to slightly above average' pupils, and 'Extension 2' was the most demanding work suitable for 'above average to most able' pupils. Pupil attainment within each level was graded A to E, but no assumption was made about the way these grades would be distributed. Thus, if a teacher felt that 60 per cent of his class deserved a 'B' in Extension 1, then that was accepted because the criteria for awarding each grade had been carefully defined by the whole department.

An important qualification on the criteria for core attainment had particular implications beyond the assessment system of the school. It was expected that *every* student should attain an 'A' grade at core level, and if this was not happening the department had to ask why. Every case where a student did not attain this grade was individually investigated and remedial action was taken. If a particular element of the core course was giving difficulties to a number of pupils, the teacher had to decide whether it was too difficult at that point in the learning sequence, or if their teaching could be changed to make it easier to understand.

It would have been an easy option to translate this well thought out approach to curriculum and teaching into a traditional report for the school to communicate its assessment of each pupil's attainment to

WHITEHILL SECONDARY SCHOOL
REPORT CARD

Name: Jimmy Smith   Class: 2c

Report No. 4   House: B

Subject	Effort Grading	Attainment Gradings			Possible 'O' Grade	Non- 'O' Grade	Written Comment
		Core	Extension 1	Extension 2			
English	A	A	A	B	✓		Keen interest in literature
Mathematics	A	A	B	B	Maths/Arith		Has an ongoing and
Geography	A	A	A	A	✓		Excellent
History	C	A	C	C		✓	Could do better
Modern Studies							
Science	B	A	C	—		✓	Distinct lack of enthusiasm
French	B	A	B	C	✓		Has some difficulty
Technical: Drawing	C	A	B	C	✓		⎫
Metalwork	C	A	C	C	✓		⎬ adequate progress
Woodwork	C	A	B	C	✓		⎭
Home Economics: Fabric							
Food							
Religious Education	D	A	C	C	—		A disruptive element in the class
Physical Education	A	A					
Music	A	A	B	B	✓		Interested
Art	A	A	B	C	✓		Shows some ability
Classical Studies							

Attendance: Number of Absences / Possible Attendances = 21 / 208

General Comments:

He has consistently attained to core in all subjects but finds difficulty in extending himself in History and Science.

A lively character, well liked by his peers although sometimes unruly in class — see Religious Education.

Date: 26/7/79   _____ Head Teacher

Figure 5.1   Whitehill Secondary School Report Card

parents. However, in Whitehill it was felt that the reduction of such diagnostic profiles to a single standardised mark was both illogical and a waste of valuable information.

The outcome, which is shown in Figure 5.1, is a compromise between detail and clarity. It recognises that different information is appropriate for diagnostic classroom use and the various forms of reporting. It was felt that detailed reporting on pupil attainment in each unit of work throughout the term would be both very demanding of valuable teacher time, and of doubtful value to the recipients of the report. The result is a fairly traditional 'academic' report of the 'tick the box' variety. Nevertheless, the reporting of subject attainment bears a close relationship to the core/extension teaching strategy. Separate grades are given under the three headings 'Core', 'Extension 1' and 'Extension 2'. The pupil who consistently attains the objectives under each heading will receive an 'A' grade, as for example Jimmy Smith has done in geography. If a pupil normally only attains the core, as is the case with Jimmy Smith's French performance, he will be given lower grades on the extension.

The important point to make about this is that no attempt is made to aggregate the scores for tests on different levels of attainment, nor are the teachers encouraged to average the scores within, for example, the extension 1 level. Instead they are expected to consult the diagnostic profile which they have built up on each student, and to award him a grade appropriate to his success in attaining what the teacher intended that he should learn, irrespective of the relative success of his classmates.

Now an Old Normgrade man might take exception to this system because it does not give the parents any idea of how the pupils are performing relative to each other. If you questioned him further, he would insist that this is essential knowledge because parents must know whether their children are ' "O" level material' and the only way they will know that is by an examination.

And in one respect the staff of Whitehill would agree with him. Parents and teachers must have information on which to make future decisions. But the teachers in Whitehill have methodically built up a diagnostic profile which provides them with ample data on which to base such a judgment. The school policy, therefore, as shown in Figure 5.1, is to present the parents, and the pupil, at the end of his second year course of study, with a recommendation for or against particular courses. This is not simply arrived at by aggregating attainment gradings. Each department holds a meeting where each student is considered, and where marginal decisions are discussed in some depth. It is a professional judgment based on carefully collected evidence which was originally used as a means of helping the student to learn, and which now informs the decision. But one would hardly expect a school which has thought out its assessment policy as carefully as Whitehill to hide behind the suspect 'objectivity' of a single standardised examination score.

The reason for looking at the termly reporting system of Whitehill High School is to highlight the way in which a school can choose to reflect its priorities in the way it communicates pupil attainment to the outside world. Chapter 6 will deal in some detail with the various ways in which 'attainment' might be reported to those seeking information on pupils leaving school, but here we will concentrate on the various possible bases for the school's day to day accountability.

School reporting of pupil attainment varies considerably in its comprehensiveness and presentation. Some schools have a long tradition of providing written reports for each pupil, others insert grades, marks or ticks in appropriate boxes, and an increasing number, like Whitehill, try to reflect something of the essential philosophy of the school in their procedure. In all cases, however, the essential purpose of the report is to communicate pupil attainment to the outside world. It is thus clear that reporting attainment in this way is simply part of the process of accountability in which schools set out their work for judgment in terms of the achievement of their pupils.

Attainment of what?

But what attainments of pupils should be reflected in school reports? There is a distinct anomaly between the stated aims of most schools, which typically include such things as the four sets of aims set out for Scottish Secondary Schools in the Munn Committee's Report which was described in Chapter 1 (page 9), and the kinds of attainment on which most schools choose to report. In many secondary schools, especially those using 'tick the box' reports, the only 'attainments' mentioned are subject grades, 'effort' and attendance. Even where open response written reports are issued, most of the comments are cryptic variants of the 'doing well/could do better' variety. Primary schools are often more adventurous in this, but even there profiles of strength and weakness are typically limited.

The Sutton Centre profile

Nevertheless, Whitehill is not unique in recognising that there needs to be a consistent logic linking classroom assessment, guidance and reporting. Another school that has thought through its reporting procedures with great care in order that they reflect and reinforce the educational policy of the school is the Sutton Centre, although it has arrived at a different kind of solution from that of Whitehill. This school's commitment is to reporting that is detailed, democratic and constructive. The comprehensive record is in the form of a profile which includes:

1 A personal section containing personal information, a record of attendance (kept by the pupil), a record of out of school activities to do with the school, and another of a pupil's independent interests and activities;

2 a general commentary by the tutor;

3 for each subject, a departmental subject summary, a teacher's comment sheet, a record of activities sheet completed by the pupil and a record of basic skills. Until recently, pupils had to decide whether or not they agreed with the teachers' comments and make resolutions which were then further commented upon by parents. Figure 5.2 gives an example.

The school has recently amended the profiles after six years' trial in order to incorporate a greater degree of freedom. This will mean that pupils can have some say in when and how the record will be kept and can choose to incorporate in it some selected pieces of work. Pupils now write first on the profile, the teacher second, the tutor for general comment third, and then it goes home to parents. In short, more emphasis is placed on the pupil's responsibility for his or her own record and less than hitherto on its use by subject teachers to communicate with parents.

A departmental approach to reporting

One of the many problems with recording and reporting achievement is to adjudicate between priorities which may, to some extent, be incompatible, such as detail and diagnosis as against clarity and comparability. For many schools the solution to these diverse strands to the recording and reporting of pupil progress is the institution of a 'multi-purpose' record. The following example is included to illustrate how one school department has recognised the partly incompatible nature of the different aspects of reporting and has sought to solve this in giving different emphases to these various aspects at different stages of a pupil's career within the overall co-ordinated assessment and reporting policy of the school. This example is particularly interesting since it shows what an individual school department can do without the prompting of the school as a whole provided it has the support of the

---

Teacher's Comments

J. must learn to discipline herself to work according to the pattern
established. She had a very slow start but has improved later and
is now making some progress. She does not find the subject easy
and will have to work really hard at it.

Signed: _E . Smith_ date: _12.12.1981_

J., within the limits of her ability, has continued to make progress.
She seems to be enjoying the work and recently has done really well.

Signed: _E. Smith_ date: _4.6 1982_

Pupil's comments

I will try to discipline myself and work harder in maths. I think
it is a fair comment.

Signed: _Joanne Jones_ date: _15.12.1981_

I am pleased with this comment and I think I do enjoy
the work we do.

Signed: _Joanne Jones_ date: _9.6.1982_

Parent's Comments

Pleased J is making some progress in this subject. I think she has
always found the subject hard.

Signed: _P. G. Jones_

Figure 5.2   An example of a Sutton Centre Profile
(Taken from C. Fletcher, 'The Sutton Centre Profile' in T. Burgess and
E. Adams (1980), *Outcomes of Education*, London, Macmillan.)

head and the governors.

The scheme developed in this particular English department takes account of both school and public examinations, personal and parents' reports, grades and statements, pupils and teachers. The main elements of the scheme are: a practical syllabus (checklist of activities and skills); teachers' reports to pupils; pupils' own programmes of work, and pupils' files which contain: a primary school record, reading age tests, graded school examination scripts and other examples of work, copies of reports to parents, and pupils' statements about themselves.[1] The department has developed a detailed set of assessment procedures to provide for communication between teacher and pupil as learning progresses. Grading is replaced by comment in the earlier years in the belief that categorising pupils undermines their ability to use assessment constructively. However, this 'non-quantitative' approach is replaced by a more explicit recognition of standard as the pupil approaches sixteen, since the department finds it necessary to work within the powerful framework of public examinations. At the same time, pupils are asked to reflect on this 'objective' evidence of their experience and competence in the subject by writing an annual 'statement' which is intended to 'strengthen their understanding of and response to "objective" assessment by giving value to subjective assessment'.[2] In this way an all-round picture of a pupil's achievement and attitude is collected, a picture which can fit into the overall profile reporting system of the school. At the same time the picture reflects both the tutor and the pupil's perspective which adds considerably to its value.

Variety within an overall policy

The teachers in the English department above were clearly fortunate in that they were able to highlight their own priorities in their reporting system. All too often, however, information on pupil attainment of the individual components of a particular area of knowledge in either primary or secondary school has to be reduced to a single grade for reporting purposes. We have seen already how assessment policies which demand this of teachers, force conformity into reporting, and that this is 'justified' in many cases by the apparent need to 'standardise' subject records for comparison. Equally, the tenor of much of this book has been to question the whole basis of assessment and reporting at a 'general attainment' level, and to advocate the assessment of specific attainments not least because this provides far richer diagnostic information.

Attendance:		
Possible: _____	**CRAIGROYSTON SCHOOL**	Student: _____
Absences: _____	1st/2nd YEAR REPORT SESSION 19 -19	House: _____ Group: _____
No. of times late: _____		Class: _____ Tutor: _____

The letter gradings in the Right Hand Columns of each subject have the following meanings: — A - Excellent; B - Above Average; C - Average; D - Below Average;
The Number gradings in the Left Hand Columns of each subject have the following meanings: — 1 - Very Good; 2 - Good; 3 - Poor; U - Unsatisfactory.

ENGLISH	
Behaviour	Spoken Eng
Effort	Listening
Progress	Reading Skill
	Spelling
	Presentation
	Imagination
OVERALL GRADING	
TEACHER	

SCIENCE	
Behaviour	Section
Effort	Introduction
Progress	Energy
Co-operation	Particles
Interest	Solvents
Care	Cells
Skill	Electricity 1
	Plants: Gases
	Heat
	Alkali : Acids
	Senses
	The Earth
	Forces
	Electricity 2
OVERALL GRADING	
TEACHER	

PHYSICAL EDUCATION	
Behaviour	Section
Interest	Gym
	Dance 1
	Dance 2
Clubs	Swimming
	Hockey
	Rugby
	Basketball
	Volleyball
	Athletics
TEACHER(S)	

MATHEMATICS & ARITHMETIC		
Behaviour	Sets I	Numbers
Effort	Co-ordinates	Fractions
Progress	Basic Algebra	Decimals
Attendance	Angles	Statistics
Homework	Negative Nos.	Soc. Arith.
	Triangles	Proportion
	Formulae	
	Inequations	
	Co-ord.Geom	
	Tr'sformat'ns	
	Sets II	
OVERALL GRADING		
TEACHER		

MODERN STUDIES	
OVERALL GRADING	
TEACHER	

ECONOMICS	
OVERALL GRADING	
TEACHER	

MAN – A COURSE OF STUDY	
Behaviour	Skills
Effort	Spoken
Interest	Written
	Practical
	Understanding
OVERALL GRADING	
TEACHER	

DRAMA	
Behaviour	Participation
Effort	Confidence
Interest	Imagination
	Expression
OVERALL GRADING	
TEACHER	

REMEDIAL DEPARTMENT EXTRACTION GROUP	
Comments	
TEACHER	

MODERN LANGUAGES	
Behaviour	Oral Work
Effort	Listening Understanding
Progress	Reading Understanding
Co-operation	
Interest	
OVERALL GRADING	
TEACHER	

TECHNICAL EDUCATION	
Behaviour	Practical
Effort	Skills
Progress	U'standing
Co-operation	Drawing
Interest	Skills
	U'standing
OVERALL GRADING	
TEACHER	

HOME ECONOMICS	
Behaviour	Cooking
Effort	Skills
Progress	U'standing
Co-operation	Sewing
Interest	Skills
Tidiness	U'standing
OVERALL GRADING	
TEACHER	

VISUAL ART	
Behaviour	Drawing
Effort	Painting
Progress	Sculpture
Co-operation	Design
Interest	Ceramics
Tidiness	
OVERALL GRADING	
TEACHER	

HISTORY	
Behaviour	Knowledge
Effort	Presentation
Progress	Imagination
Co-operation	
Interest	
OVERALL GRADING	
TEACHER	

GEOGRAPHY	
Behaviour	Knowledge
Effort	Reasoning
Progress	Written Work
Co-operation	Map Work
Interest	
OVERALL GRADING	
TEACHER	

MUSIC	
Behaviour	Pract. Work
Effort	Written Work
Progress	
Co-operation	
Interest	
OVERALL GRADING	
TEACHER	
INSTRUMENT INSTRUCTION	

Subject Teachers' Comments:	Group Tutor's Comments:

DEPARTMENTAL RECOMMENDATIONS	Parent's Signature:	Date of next Parents' meeting

E	A	M	F	Ge	T	HE	Mu	H	G	MS	C	P	B	Art

is: _____

House Director's Comments:

(Headteacher)

Date: _____

Figure 5.3   *Craigroyston School 1st/2nd Year Report*

Inevitably, however, recognition of the importance of assessment related to component parts of a school subject can create considerable problems at the reporting stage. These problems are not unsurmountable, however. Figure 5.3 shows an example of how one school has designed its own report sheet to allow *both* for variety among subjects in their reporting, whilst retaining the coherence of an overall school reporting policy.

The first interesting point to note is that in every subject, with the exception of Modern Studies, Economics (and perhaps, 'Remedial'), the teacher is expected to assess pupil performance in a number of affective areas such as 'behaviour', 'effort' and 'interest'. Significantly departments have been given freedom to extend this list considerably, and even greater freedom is given in the right-hand column. In this, each department has set out a number of areas on which it provides information on pupil attainment of specific subject related components. Thus, in visual art, separate information can be made available on drawing, painting, sculpture, design and ceramics, while in science, the information provided relates to overall attainment of specific parts of the course such as 'electricity', 'heat', 'forces', and so on.

Clearly there is considerable variation amongst the subjects in what the teachers have decided that it is important to communicate to parents. Equally, criticisms might be made of what has been chosen by a number of departments, and it would be interesting to discover how the choice was arrived at. Indeed, all of the reporting systems at which we have looked could be criticised on a number of grounds, both theoretical and practical. But in every case the reality of the situation is that when the compromise is made amongst clarity, depth and time, something has to be left out. The comprehensive reporting account provided by Craigroyston is just one example of how the compromise has been reached. Its importance, like the other examples described in this chapter, lies first and foremost in its recognition that the style and content of reporting demand just as much careful attention and planning as every other aspect of assessment within the school.

A place for parents

Even from these brief examples it is not hard to see that the types of attainment and the ways in which they are reported can vary substantially from school to school. What they have in common is an attempt to combine the ethos of the schools' internal assessment policy with the ways in which it manifests pupil attainment so that they can produce reports which communicate much more efficiently than hitherto with parents and pupils.

But many schools have not faced up to these questions. They are still sending home the traditional stereotyped report which simply contains a list of subjects and a space for grades and/or percentages.[3] Often there is no space at all for teachers' comments on behaviour or progress. Frequently such comments as are included are distinctly unhelpful and we are all familiar with the 'fair', 'could do better', 'disappointing' kind of comment, if not with the more outrageous 'who is he?' or simply 'ugh'! None of these comments is in any way constructive and such an attitude to reporting on the part of the school frequently requires it to engage in elaborate procedures to circumvent reports being lost, defaced or otherwise tampered with on their way home.

Equally, it is still rare for parents to be invited to comment on a report as at the Sutton Centre or to come to school to discuss it. Even at the crucial stage in secondary school of subject choice for certificate courses, parents may simply be informed of the proposed course options for their child[4] and may, or may not, be invited to discuss these proposals or to help their child in making such decisions.

This brings us to the thorny question of parent and pupil access to records, an issue which has been the focus of much controversy in the United States.[5] Argued calmly and logically, the case for parents to have complete access to records would seem irrefutable,[6] but there is evidence of a substantial body of opinion which regards the keeping of confidential records within the school as a necessary part of teacher professionalism without which it would be impossible to record relevant personal information about pupils and their family circumstances.[7] It is not for us to adjudicate in this issue. Rather, our task is to offer for your consideration examples of approaches to reporting which you may · find helpful in thinking about the kind of relationship you wish to foster with parents.

Or, as a parent, you may see the issue from the other side and be thinking about the kinds of feedback and involvement you want to have in 'keeping track of teaching'. To some extent the range of options open to you to press for are determined by the ethos and the leadership of the individual school concerned. This will be manifest in the strength of its Parent Teacher Association and, indeed, whether this exists at all. It will also be manifest in the role played by governors, particularly parent governors. If you are unfortunate enough to be sending your child to one of the surprisingly large number of schools which bear a sign 'Parents must not pass this point', you have a long struggle ahead of you if you wish to convince the school of the benefit of involving parents at every stage of children's learning. It is to be hoped that siege tactics of this kind will become increasingly rare. Sadly, it is equally likely that the current climate of accountability which is subjecting teachers to increasing pressure from both the community below and the educational hierarchy above is just as likely to encourage this kind of defensiveness.

Given that a child only spends about six hours out of twenty-four at school, the argument for parents and teachers to work together in providing mutual feedback is indisputable. Equally, it must be recognised that for most teachers report-writing is currently a time-consuming and unrewarding chore. Good reporting cannot but be time-consuming and time must be found in the already over-full school calendar for it to be done properly. It does not need to be unrewarding, however. The key lies in the kind of approach to assessment, recording and reporting which is the theme of this book in which such 'chores' become an integral and vital part of teaching. Each school will find its own way of doing this according to its priorities and its curriculum organisation. For some it will be a profile sheet giving grades for achievement in the various different aspects of each subject. Other schools use a comment sheet for each subject which is collated into a report book. A few others, like the Sutton Centre, may incorporate a space for pupils to comment before the report goes home and another space for parents to add their comments. Whatever their form, such reports ought to be essentially diagnostic, documenting the strengths and weaknesses of the pupil, making constructive suggestions and inviting equally a constructive response from pupil and parent.

It is important too if these reports are not to be a chore, that they are an integral, not an extra part of the school's approach to record keeping as a whole. In most of the examples discussed in this chapter the information to be sent to parents was readily available in existing records and, equally, the feedback received from parents was incorporated in the cumulative record. Apart from the benefits better communication can bring, a closer relationship between school and home will, we believe, be beneficial psychologically in fostering a greater sense of community and shared commitment on the part of teacher and parent.

Attainments of schools or attainments of pupils?

Until now this chapter has focused on how teachers and schools might communicate their assessment of the attainment of pupils to interested parties. The thought must have passed through the minds of many pupils and parents, however, that it might be equally appropriate to set exams for teachers in schools as regularly as they are applied to pupils. As we will see when the work of the Assessment of Performance Unit of the Department of Education and Science, and the issue of publishing external examination results are discussed below under the heading 'External criteria for accountability', many schools feel that such a movement has already begun. An interesting outcome of these moves has been to heighten the awareness of the teaching profession of their responsibility to be accountable, and to open the debate on what goes on in schools to a wider public. Needless to say, the question of just how to go about this is a considerable headache for teachers, and head teachers, but amongst the most promising approaches from within the school is to adopt a policy of self-evaluation.

School self-evaluation

Essentially the argument is as follows. Given that there is an acceptance of the *need* to communicate more about the achievement of the school and its pupils to parents, governing bodies, local authorities and the community in general, which model of evaluation might a school adopt? To keep matters simple, we will consider briefly two alternatives; a 'product' model and a 'process' model. In the product model the assumption is made that there is a clear relationship between the inputs to the system (pupils, teachers, teaching materials, time, etc.) and the output, which can be thought of as pupils who have changed in some way. Furthermore, it is assumed that the types of changes which will occur will be specified in advance, pupil attainment of these changes can be measured, and the 'success' or 'failure' of the system can be evaluated in terms of such pupil attainment as takes place. These assumptions lend themselves to the monitoring process of the Assessment of Performance Unit which we will discuss below.

At the other extreme, the process model focuses on the way schools function within given circumstances. In the view, for example, of Macdonald[8] there is a profundity of ignorance about many aspects of what goes on in learning which makes it difficult to evaluate 'success' in terms of easily measured outcomes. He states that:

> we do not understand the learning process very well. We do not
> know for sure what causes learning . . . we do not know what causes
> the successful learning . . . we suspect that what students learn
> is the product of many social and biological forces which interact
> in ways we dimly apprehend but cannot quantify in even a single
> case so that we are unable to isolate the contribution of the school.

Now where this assumption is made about the functioning of school systems, it becomes difficult to conceptualise 'success' or 'failure' in terms of pupil 'outputs' unless these are set within a much more comprehensive framework of understanding the 'process'. Furthermore, most aspects of the process cannot be 'measured' in the normal sense and have to be 'evaluated' either by outside observers or, as is the suggestion in the school self-evaluation approach, by the school itself.

The argument between those who hold views at either extreme of the product-process continuum will no doubt continue for a long time to come, but it seems to us, that the notion of school self-evaluation has much to offer teachers and schools who are interested either in looking more critically at the way in which they function at the present time, or who want to consider as objectively as possible how new approaches in the classroom might affect them. And while reaction against the concept of externally controlled accountability is often seen as the reason for schools adopting self-evaluation, we would endorse Simons's[9] suggestion that: 'Professionalism should be the major justification . . . not response to a short term political demand'. But what does a school self-evaluation look like? The outcome might, in fact, be a document the length of this book. A better notion of its content can be had, for example, by looking at a list of the sort of information which could be included put forward by Macdonald:[10]

Routine information of the following kind might be collected:
1   Names, qualifications and relevant occupational experience of the staff and their institutional responsibilities
2   Similar information about local advisers and HMIs in regular touch with the school
3   Similar information about the Board of Governors
4   Information about the systems of appointment for staff and governors
5   Information about how to lodge a complaint against the school and about the school's procedure for dealing with complaints
6   Disciplinary policy and procedures for grievance
7   Information about the decision making processes of the school in relation to the distribution of responsibilities, internal forms of accountability and the procedures for reviewing practice
8   Rules for staff and pupils
9   Information about school policy with regard to the promotion of academic attainment, social life, pastoral care and health indicating how these policies are reflected in the organisation

of the school and the curriculum and the allocation of resources

10 Information about pupil assessment, pupil records and examination policy and career guidance

11 Public examination results

12 Information about liaison with feeder schools and other schools or institutions of education which the school itself feeds

13 Information about liaison with parents

14 Information about income and expenditure for the current year

15 Information about staff development policy

16 Information about extra curricular activities, links with the community, links with community bodies, etc

17 Information about provision for remedial teaching and professional qualifications of the staff responsible

18 Information about involvement with educational experiments, innovation, etc.

Further inclusions might cover more detailed information from individual departments about the content of their syllabuses, teaching styles adopted, outcomes expected of the learning process and (to fire a shot across the bow of those who see the process and product models as being mutually exclusive), evidence of the extent to which these intended outcomes are being achieved.

Now such an exercise must appear daunting in the extreme to many who approach it for the first time. Furthermore, as Vernava[11] points out the outcome can be little more than a bureaucratic exercise unless it is carried out with the clear intention of doing something about observed deficiences. The analogy with the tension between assessment for reporting and assessment for diagnosis in the classroom springs immediately to mind. School self-evaluation has, however, been encouraged by a number of local education authorities.[12] That produced by Solihull is amongst the most detailed. It covers a comprehensive range of school activity as Table 5.1 shows, its intention being to provide a framework for schools in their efforts to clarify objectives and priorities, in identifying weaknesses and strengths, and in ensuring that any due attention is given to all aspects of school life.

So thorough is the list of areas of potential concern that working through even one sub-section — such as that shown below on 'Pupil Assessment, record-keeping and reporting' — has been found to take a group of teachers anything up to a year. This extract shows the

TABLE 5.1   *Contents of the Solihull School Self-Evaluation Scheme*

A EVALUATING ORGANISATION AND MANAGEMENT: a
framework for evaluating the organisational and management work
of the school as a whole, of groups of staff such as departmental and
pastoral teams, and of the work of individual staff in their
organisational and management roles.
  1 Objective Setting
  2 Planning (a) General Considerations
            (b) Staff Recruitment, Selection, Allocation of
                  Tasks and Development
            (c) The Provision and Use of Material Resources
                  and Finance
            (d) The Sequence and Timing of Activities
  3 Decision Making
  4 Distribution of Responsibility and Authority
  5 Group and Personal Relations, Motivation and Morale
  6 Communication, including Routine Administration
  7 Co-ordinating and Supervising the System
  8 Evaluation and Review of a Working Group
B EVALUATING SPECIFIC ASPECTS OF THE SCHOOL'S WORK
  1 The Curriculum
  2 The Pastoral System
  3 School 'Climate' and Discipline
  4 Extra-Curricular Arrangements
  5 Health and Safety
  6 The Library
  7 Careers, and Further and Higher Education Guidance
  8 Pupil Assessment, Record Keeping and Reporting
  9 The School's External Relations with
            (a) Community
            (b) Parents
            (c) Other Educational Establishments
            (d) Education Office and Welfare Agencies
 10 Some Useful Statistics
C FURTHER ANALYSIS OF TEACHERS' ROLES
  1 Analysing the Subject Teacher's Work
  2 Analysing the Teacher's Pastoral Role
  3 Analysing the Teacher's Role as a Member of the School
     and of the Teaching Profession
D IN-SERVICE EDUCATION AND STAFF DEVELOPMENT
     Response Sheet for In-Service Enquiry
  1 Curricular Aspects
  2 Pastoral Aspects
  3 General and Inter-Departmental Aspects
  4 Services Offered by External Agents
     Sample Evaluation Response Sheets

criteria offered in the document under one sub-heading which can form a basis for a school's own self-evaluation.

B8 Pupil Assessment, Record Keeping and Reporting

1 Pupil progress is carefully monitored by reliable tests.
2 There is effective discussion and guidance on the purpose and methods of assessment.
3 Tests are carefully designed to test objectives set in terms of knowledge, skills, application which are agreed to be important.
4 An appropriate variety of tests and evaluation methods is used: standardised achievement tests, diagnostic tests, continuous assessment methods.
5 Assessment methods are used effectively to diagnose the needs and problems of individual pupils.
6 Assessment results, are, when required, properly standardised to allow meaningful comparisons to be made.
7 Pupils' work is checked carefully and frequently.
8 Marking and assessment are used constructively to direct and/or motivate pupils and to improve their performance.
9 Pupils with particular problems are helped immediately.
10 Reports are legible, clearly expressed and free of errors.
11 Reports are full and detailed.
12 Reports are designed to improve appreciation of pupils' strengths and weaknesses for the benefit of parents and the pupils themselves.
13 Reports indicate ways of improving performance.
14 Time is devoted by staff to discussing report writing. Guidance is given.
15 Record cards are clear, systematic and detailed.
16 Records of pupil performance and progress are efficiently stored and accessible.
17 Record cards are kept up to date and are accurate and detailed.
18 The records include details relating to the school's objectives.

We have deliberately included this particular aspect of school concern as our example of a pro forma for school self-evaluation since it raises issues of more general concern which are the subject of this book. The eighteen evaluation criteria listed here clearly reflect a set of 'assessment principles' such as the integration of assessment with teaching, diagnostic feedback, standardisation and comprehensiveness of scope. As such, they echo many of the themes of this book. What the criteria do not do, however, is provide any *overall* policy or rationale as a basis for these exhortations. Without such a justification, the choice of these criteria must seem arbitrary, imposing a set of priorities on teachers with regard to assessment that they may not share. Even if the criteria are agreed, this is only the beginning of the thorny process of reconciling contradictory imperatives which, this book suggests, is likely to characterise the development of a school assessment policy.

Indeed, such contradictions in a specific policy area are illustrative of the kinds of problem inherent in school self-evaluation in general. The degree of 'success' — however measured — varies considerably from school to school, but Simons,[13] reporting on her experience with several groups of teachers (over 200 in all), from both primary and secondary schools, has noted a number of conditions which seem likely to contribute to success. Amongst these is that:

> The group initiative is likely to be more sustained than an individual one and the results considered more seriously . . . that the climate in the school is ideally one in which everyone is a potential contributor and everyone is committed to reviewing the findings as a basis for decision making . . . and that starting small is important if evaluation is to be instituted as part of a continuing process. Large scale evaluations involving massive data gathering and long reports tend to be seen as a one off exercise which, once completed, need no further attention.

This last point draws our attention to the question of how school self-evaluation might be used. At the first level of application proposed by, for example, Macdonald,[14] and Simons,[15] such introspection can be invaluable data on which to base a review of school policy, teaching methodology and curriculum, not least if the staff are committed to it. As progress is made, and as the staff become less apprehensive of the exercise, so the contents of such a self-evaluation might be made public.

It would be difficult to argue that a school which made such information available to parents and local authorities had not taken its responsibility to be accountable seriously. And, equally, it would be far less easy for schools to be compared on crude data about pupil attainment of basic skills when such a comprehensive picture of the whole process of education is available for inspection.

External criteria for accountability

Inevitably, though, the notion of a school making itself accountable in its own terms to the society of which it is part runs into obstacles and the demand for more formal bases for comparability. The decentralised nature of education in Britain has tended to exacerbate such demands. Traditionally it has fallen to Her Majesty's Inspectorate, now an increasingly important agent of policy-making in education, to be the bastion of comparative standards amongst schools. In recent years as the power of HMI actually to enforce standards has diminished, there has been a corresponding increase in pressure for other, often less subtle, methods of imposing accountability from without the school.

External examinations as indices

Perhaps the most obvious and superficially attractive means of imposing accountability from outside the school is to use the results of external examinations sat by pupils, to make comparisons amongst schools. A great institution of academic one-upmanship amongst some sectors of education, is the annual *Times Educational Supplement* League Table of the number of pupils obtaining scholarships to the universities of Oxford and Cambridge. A suggestion of the problems which might arise from using this method of comparison elsewhere in the educational system might be gained by reflecting on the trauma faced by the head teacher of Joe Bloggs's Comprehensive, who is asked by one pupil for special tuition in Greek, mathematics and astronomy in the third year sixth, to allow him to enter for an Oxbridge Scholarship. Clearly, this would present a dilemma to a head teacher, in the adequate allocation of resources between such 'high fliers' to whom a disproportionate amount of staffing must be given in comparison with the general needs of the bulk of the school population. Yet when the layman comes to compare school results in the same way as he might compare football teams, it is likely that he will be more impressed by the success of the few than the undistinguished but commendable progress of the many.

In essence then, the opponents of using the results of external examinations to compare schools, argue that the great variety of factors which influence school results makes it extremely difficult to interpret the outcomes. Schools vary in many ways including their catchment areas, their staff turnover rates, the facilities and infra-structure available to them, their truancy rates, the commitment of their staff, and in their policy in deciding who should be presented for given external examinations. Consequently, it does not follow that 'poor' examination results reflect 'poor' teaching. A school which serves a catchment area, where the parental contribution to encouraging pupil success is low, which has high truancy rates, but which has a liberal policy in allowing as many pupils as possible to be presented for 'O' grade examination, may have a very low pass rate per pupil, while a school in the same town which serves an educationally conscious parent population may procure an extremely high pass rate per pupil by severely restricting the number of pupils it enters. However, the teaching in the former school might be extremely enlightened even to the point of giving pupils so much individual attention that they are enabled to overcome problems stemming from factors outside the control of the teacher, while in the latter school a staid 'academic' policy of examination-oriented teaching without taking real responsibility for pupils' academic progress, could result in the same pupils falling by the wayside at an early stage. The question, of course, is to what extent comparison by external examination can help parents to make appropriate choices for their children.

The implications of publishing league tables for comparison, which present teachers with the greatest challenge, however, concerns how teachers will react to them. Samuel[16] spells out the issues when he suggests that:

> In broad terms schools can provide what the public wants. Over a generation of pupils, teachers can adapt sufficiently to begin to achieve the aims which the public demands. In reacting to their perceptions of public opinion, they may well change the direction of schools in a way that parents might not necessarily want.

> Unfortunately, there is a tendency for the examinable to drive out the unexaminable . . . . If we arrive at the stage where in classes streamed for ability, the brightest pupils are taught by the best or most experienced teachers, while the less able are instructed by staff of lower calibre, is this what the public really wants? Is it compatible with the concept basic to comprehensive schools that the education of every child must be regarded as of equal value?

It is thus clear that the publication of results takes schools into the political arena. Not only do teachers, and society in general, have to contend with issues such as those put forward by Samuel, but at a more local level, education committees will have to deal with thorny implications such as whether 'poor' results means that more or less resources should be provided for schools, whether school catchment areas and intakes should be manipulated in an attempt to redress 'results' inequalities, and in an era of potential school closures, whether such information should have any bearing on decisions as to which school should go.

From a professional standpoint, however, the weight of the argument would seem to be that the information which these superficial comparisons can provide is inadequate. In a political situation where

105

publication of public examination results is mandatory, it is essential that such results are read within the context of adequate accounting from within the school. At least in this context, accountability from within and outside the school are complementary.

Monitoring by item bank

Another way of providing for accountability from outside the school is the use of 'item banks'. It is recognised that item banks are a useful source of 'expertly' produced tests for diagnostic purposes which can be of considerable value to teachers in making diagnostic assessments, if used carefully. As we will see here, the alternative use of item banks for national or local monitoring is a more contentious issue.

The idea of applying tests on a large scale with a view to surveying national attainment amongst school children is not new. The National Foundation for Educational Research began testing reading performance in 1948. The Scottish Council for Research in Education carried out tests of English and Arithmetic on over 72,000 ten-year-olds in 1953, and since 1969 the National Assessment of Educational Progress programme in the United States has carried out large scale surveys of a considerable variety of attainments amongst nine-, thirteen- and seventeen-year-olds and young adults. Similarly, the monitoring of attainment at a local level has been practised widely especially in the United States, and in Britain at a research level[17] and is LEA policy in a number of areas.[18]

In this tradition, and amidst a flurry of political concern about 'standards of achievement' amongst school-leavers, an Assessment of Performance Unit was set up in 1974 by the Department of Education and Science: 'To promote the development of assessing and monitoring the achievement of children at school and to seek to identify the incidence of under achievement.' The Assessment of Performance Unit is concerned in principle with the changing levels of attainment of certain basic standards at a national level. This is to be carried out by periodic samples of pupil performance using only a small proportion of the school population taken from throughout the country. Originally the Unit set out to monitor standards of attainment in language (native and foreign), mathematics, science, personal and social development, aesthetic development and physical development. Progress has been ˸ow, however, on aesthetic, personal and social development and it ˸ well be that the reports of the Unit come to focus only on ˸ge, maths and science where surveys have already taken place.

˸rallel to this has been the development at the NFER of the

Local Education Authorities and Schools Item Banks (LEASIB) project which is seen as having two potential uses; monitoring and attainment testing. LEASIB must be thought of as a first cousin of the APU, if for no other reason than that the NFER who are also responsible for the work being carried out in maths and language[19] state that: 'the "broad comparability" of the results obtained with the LEASIB material with that of the results obtained by the APU will be studied in order that the most meaningful comparisons may be made by the LEA concerned.'

The basic notion is that the LEAs and perhaps individual schools will have access to a bank of tests initially in mathematics and language but potentially extending to other areas at a later date.

Since the initiation of these activities 'APU bashing' and bolstering have become a popular pastime at a number of levels. Our attention here is not to make any judgment on this debate, but to attempt to pick out the main arguments in the two questions 'What is to be tested?' and 'How useful is the information?' and consider them in the context of how the practising teacher might cope with the resulting dilemma. What we will not do is enter into the argument about the technical approaches to item analysis which are complicated and inconclusive.[20]

What is to be tested?

There is a fairly reasonable assumption that within the arithmetic taught in any two primary schools, or the science taught in any two secondary schools, there is an underlying common core. But once one moves beyond this fairly limited area of knowledge or takes in less comparable areas of study such as art, local studies, history and indeed much of mathematics, it is far less easy to argue that there is a consensus of what a teacher expects a pupil to learn by a certain age, or indeed learn at all. For those who attempt to monitor pupil attainment this creates enormous headaches.[21] Most basic is that a test which covers only a small common core is unlikely to do justice to the wide range of learning outcomes expected by any single teacher. At the national level this means that there is considerable danger of appearing to be making comments on the school system as a whole when many of the contextual variables (such as those used in school self reports) may have changed, or when standards of attainment amongst those parts of learning *not* sampled by the tests are just as important.

And while such misrepresentations at a national level are likely only to affect the classroom teacher through reading erroneous press headlines, at the local level, application and misinterpretation of similar (narrow) tests using LEASIB or other item banks could have much more immediate consequences. Thus, for example, Taylor[22] describes how in one local authority use of the 'Carver Reading Test for all eight year olds under the direction of the County Remedial Team . . . (gave) at least some information on which to base judgements about allocation of resources, particularly of remedial teachers, other than hunch', and in the United States standardised achievement tests have been used widely to make judgments about resource allocation often with highly questionable results.

Knowing that the result of monitoring tests can contribute to such judgments has a number of consequences. A considerable danger is that teachers will come to direct their curriculum to the content of the tests which they feel to be examining *their* competence as much as the attainment of their pupils. And while this might have positive benefits in improving the teaching of the relatively incompetent, it will at the same time detract from the effort many teachers put into teaching for other, often *more* important, learning outcomes.

In brief, then, national and, even more important, local monitoring activities can distort the total picture of what is happening in schools and can exercise a disturbing backwash effect on the curriculum. If the inadequacies of the approach are not recognised then we have an example of how assessment can potentially endanger the varied activities of the modern classroom. On the other hand, it can be argued that, used intelligently and seen within the whole context of possibly more important aspects of a school's activities, such information could well be a bonus to the teacher who wants to monitor her own success in teaching her pupils.

How useful is the information on standards?

But just how useful is such information to the classroom teacher? How relevant is it? Nuttall,[23] for example, notes that amongst the items used to test pupil knowledge of word meaning in a language test used both in 1954 and in a recent HMI primary survey were 'mannequin', 'haber-dashers' and 'wheelwright'. Now while we will assume that the current tests of the APU, LEASIB and similar organisations will be more discriminating in their choice of items, in the long term someone has to make a decision on which content is relevant to the then current circumstances.

But essentially this point is nit-picking when used against the wider context of relevance. Dockrell,[24] for example, suggests that:

It is arguable that what parents and employers and others need is not more information of a general kind about standards, but a better understanding of what it is that schools are setting out to achieve, and how particular activities fit into these objectives. Employers need to know as a basis for discussion with educational authorities what arithmetic the schools are trying to teach, and what communication skills are being taught. Parents need to know that apparently random play activities in primary 1, or field studies in secondary 4 are carefully thought out parts of an overall programme making a specified contribution to the children's learning. They also need to be assured that the schools their own children attend are providing the same opportunities as are available to others. Surveys of national standards will not inform them on either of these points.

Of course, it can be argued that while this sort of information may be important to parents and others, it is not the information which national surveys of achievement are intended to provide. Instead, as Selby[25] tells us:

The reports [of the APU] will be statements of fact describing the performance of the national samples of pupils in relation to single items or groups of items. In the first instance, these reports will give a first ever national profile of performance to which subsequent reports may be related in order to describe any detectable changes in performance as time goes by. The performance described will be related to the variables like school size and location, which have been used to draw a balanced sample, but no causal relationships can be assumed.

But again we must ask ourselves how useful information on national standards in discrete areas of the curriculum might be. Returning again to Dockrell, who asks:

how would a particular teacher know whether to move attention which it is held should be paid nationally to the layout of short division sums applied to his class. If he was already providing more attention than the average, should he provide not more, but perhaps less. Is it likely that those already giving considerable attention to the layout of short division sums would feel strengthened in their conviction and provide even more? Would those not giving sufficient attention have overlooked this point in the recommendations of the report? Findings from national survey may or may not apply to any particular teacher, and whether any teachers will take account of them will depend very much on their own values and their own perception of their current practice.

In fact, what we get down to is the fact stressed throughout the book, but especially in chapter 3, that the most useful information to the teacher relates to the success or failure of her own classes, or individual pupils within these classes, in attaining what she set out to teach them. And in relation to external monitoring this creates the peculiar anomaly that the most useful information on standards will not come from the national monitoring of the APU, but from local or individual school use of LEASIB, which, as we have already seen, is the type of monitoring most likely to distort her success or failure if it concentrates only on a narrow band of attainment. The teacher who does not take note of these issues when trying to make sense of the attempts of others outside her classroom to monitor the achievement of her pupils is thus in danger of falling blindly into the trap of narrowing her own perspective. The teacher who approaches monitoring with knowledge of the dangers of reading more into it than can be warranted by the limited scope of the exercise can probably use the outcomes to the advantage of her teaching and her pupils' learning. The question of whether those who are commissioning such exercises have done enough to allow teachers to come to terms with both the potential and the limitations remains unanswered, as does the question of whether those outside the schools and the classrooms can be relied upon to treat the outcomes with the delicacy demanded. One cannot help but recall the experience in the State of Michigan where the test scores of individual schools were published after the teachers had been assured that they would remain confidential.[26] Small surprise that Bleecher,[27] found that teachers in Michigan regarded the State accountability system as:

1 Inconsistent with the purposes of the school organisation as they understood them;
2 Not compatible with their personal interests;
3 Not able to be complied with mentally and physically.

Conclusions

In entering into the problem of accountability and the relationships between establishment bodies and the classroom teacher we have moved far beyond the technical considerations which typify the content of most contemporary books on assessment. Yet if the teacher is to make decisions for her own classroom or her own school, on what is the most appropriate approach for the modern classroom, she inevitably makes decisions which have a 'knock-on' effect throughout the educational system. In the same way, government decisions to set up monitoring bodies, or to enforce the publication of external examination results for schools, have inevitable consequences for the classroom teacher. Assessment is at the sharp end of the political interface between school and society[28] and, in a climate where schools are no longer accepted as unchanging repositories and dispensaries of the nation's knowledge, it would be naive to assume that those outside the school will simply accept what they are given without question. The last few decades have seen a move in schools towards emphasising the development of the pupil as an inquiring and critical member of society. In these terms those working in the educational system should perhaps see the increasing public interest in the performance of schools — expressed as a concern for accountability — as an unforeseen but desirable outcome of these intentions. We would have failed to educate our pupils in the skills of inquiry and criticism if, in turn, the educational system itself did not come to be questioned.

But what are the practical consequences of this for the teacher in the modern classroom? We have seen that in making reports on pupil attainment to parents, and indeed to the pupils themselves, schools can reflect their own priorities and culture and the particular strengths of their teaching staff. But what are these priorities and strengths? Who determines them? Are they implicit or explicit? Do they derive from received and historical tablets, or are they negotiated and dynamic? The onus is on teachers at all levels of the school hierarchy to be aware of the variety of decisions which might be made at this basic level of accountability.

Moving a stage further the teacher is still intimately concerned with the decision-making process if the school chooses to enter into the realm of school self-evaluation. Introspection on the adequacy of one's teaching strategies, curriculum and assessment policy are inevitable concomitants of serious school self-evaluation, and in consequence, accountability may come to suggest change and professional growth. How does one allow teachers to prepare for this? What support is necessary to sustain such growth? What structures, both within schools and local education authorities, at a decision-making level and in the realm of consultancy are required? Again, unless adequate consideration is given to these issues by the teachers themselves, the whole notion of self-evaluation will, at best, result in wasted effort, and, at worst, lay schools open to unqualified crude comparison by superficial measurement.

111

Finally, in dealing with the problems of accountability from outside the school, the priority for practising teachers must again be awareness of the issues. It could be argued that a teacher working in a school which has a clearly thought out internal accountability policy has little to fear from external comparisons, and indeed, might be in a position to make wise use of some such information in deciding her own priorities. However, as we have seen in this chapter, such data must be treated with caution, and this underlines the need for teachers to know how to deal with it in their own classroom context.

None of these tensions, constraints, conflicts and issues is essentially new. Nor indeed are the notions of monitoring and accountability alien to a teaching situation which constantly monitors the progress of its pupils. The danger is in the potential distortion of the outcomes of the process. The answer from a professional standpoint must be a careful consideration of its implications by everyone involved in any sector of the educational system.

Chapter 6

And so to work ...
the final reckoning

At first sight, it may seem inappropriate that a book subtitled 'assessment in the modern classroom' should have a chapter on reporting on the final outcomes of a pupil's time in school. Decisions about what to report, when and how, are typically outside the control of the classroom teacher and thus, arguably, fall outside the concerns of this book. In fact, we must reiterate the point made in chapter 5 that no book on any aspect of school assessment can legitimately ignore this area because it is in its choice of what to communicate to the outside world – to parents, to other educational institutions, and in particular to employers – that a school most clearly reveals the aims and values that inform its work as a whole.

In fact 'reporting' is an umbrella term which includes several different sorts of communication. First, there is reporting to pupils to give them feedback on their progress and to help them make decisions about future courses and aspirations. The emphasis here will differ from the most well-known aspect of reporting – the periodic communication of a pupil's progress to his parents. Both these activities will differ from the third sort of reporting which is concerned with passing information about school-leavers to interested parties – further and higher education and potential employers – in the outside world. And while pupils and many parents will probably be quite ready to take the school's assessment at its face value, this last group is likely to place considerable emphasis on the clarity of the report which they receive, the validity of the assertions which it makes and its relevance to what they see as their particular concerns.

The impetus for change

However, as preceding chapters of this book have demonstrated, a good deal of the information contained in traditional school reports is at worst misleading and incomplete and at best, negative or stereotyped. The impetus towards change in school reporting has come from two sources. One stimulus has been the major changes that have taken place in recent years in classroom organisation, curriculum and pedagogy in many schools. The new demands which this has placed on assessment have equally been the stimulus for this book. In a climate of such wide ranging re-examination of aims and methods, assessment and reporting could not and have not remain unaffected as the study of Whitehill in chapter 5 clearly illustrates.

The other stimulus has been the greatly increased numbers of pupils now staying on in secondary schools until they are sixteen. Partly but not wholly as a result of the raising of the school-leaving age in 1972, many pupils are now in school at the 'O' level stage for whom 'O' level and even CSE may be neither a suitable nor an attainable goal. The frequently disruptive presence of these pupils in schools has led to a whole series of initiatives aimed at developing a school-leaving certificate which will be a valid and reliable basis for communicating information about the pupil to interested parties outside the school and so provide an attainable and worthwhile goal for such pupils to pursue. The overwhelming problem in devising formal reports at this level is that in terms of the traditional 'academic' terms of most schools, many of these pupils would receive little more than a record of failure. And yet many pupils have positive and useful attributes which are not assessed in the conventional context. Add to this the necessity for comparability between teachers, between departments and between schools which even the sophistication of the examination boards working with what appear to be 'measurable' variables has not yet been totally able to master, and the difficulties in developing such a new approach to reporting are readily apparent.

In this chapter we shall concentrate particularly upon school-leaving reports, but it is worth noting that there is no better way of pointing out the crucial issues to be faced in deciding what information ought to be the content of reports to parents at earlier stages in a pupil's progress through school than by discussing these issues in the much more controversial context of terminal school reports.

Equally, if terminal reports are to be worthwhile, they too must be part of the cumulative process of assessment and dialogue which has accompanied a pupil's progress up the school. If not, the production of the requisite information will impose a severe assessment burden on teachers or, in all probability, reduce the scope of the report to the results of a 'one-off' formal test or highly impressionistic comment.

Thus, just as one of the main themes of this book is the need to integrate assessment procedures with curriculum practice, so it is important to note that the issues considered in this chapter should not be dealt with in isolation from what we have looked at earlier in the book. What has typically happened is that curriculum practice has rather tended to follow the dictates of formal assessment. This need not be the case with the new kinds of terminal report now being developed, since they can be designed as an integral part of curriculum activity. This will only be possible where there is as much willingness to think radically about the curriculum as about assessment.

It is widely acknowledged that a good deal of the traditional fare of schooling is quite unsuitable for the majority of youngsters, but whilst a plethora of work experience, link courses and other kinds of vocational training reflect this concern, it has so far made little impact on the assumptions that underpin educational provision and the organisational arrangements which they sustain. Thus, courses are still designed for pupils, rather than pupils participating in their organisation. Teaching is still overwhelmingly verbal and didactic, assessment is almost exclusively formal and written and done to pupils. It is a question beyond the scope of this book in what way educational priorities should be changing but what is of relevance is the fact that almost without exception, those advocating reforms in reporting see it as necessarily accompanied by some degree of equivalent change in educational goals and procedures.[1]

One of the most well-known reformers in this field, Don Stansbury,[2] has written:

> the kind of education that we have now to an amazing degree in
> our secondary schools prepares the young very well for the
> technology of the nineteenth century . . . changes in technology
> associated with the microprocessor revolution require a different
> kind of education one that puts the main emphasis on the
> development of personal qualities, that encourages differences and
> that values enterprise, energy and self-confidence . . . what people
> need to offer are the distinctively human capacities like the capacity
> to plan, to choose, to decide, to respond to the unexpected.

Stansbury argues that it is our failure to equip pupils in this way, far more than economic decline or the silicon chip, which has led to the bleak figures for youth unemployment both in this country and abroad. Teenage unemployment has been rising at three times the general level of unemployment since 1972 and stood in mid-1980 at 281,900 — an increase of nearly 40 per cent on 1979's already peak figure. The stark meaning of this statitic is that in 1980 one out of two school-leavers went straight into unemployment.[3] In 1982 prospects are even worse.

Without a major change in direction, schools are likely to continue preparing large numbers of their pupils for idleness and failure.[4]

> Young people are likely to spend much of . . . their waking hours in what we call peer-groups, which is to say, gangs of people about their own age. Since this sub-culture has no useful work to do, and is cut off from any of the serious concerns and purposes of adult life, it becomes a sub-culture obsessed with consumption, status, show, like a society of decadent aristocrats. It tends to produce young people, who with very few exceptions, must be unique in history in their sense of their own — and by extension, everyone else's — worthlessness. These young people are both a great (and needless) tragedy, and a great danger since they are perfect raw material for any kind of violent, nihilist, neo-Fascist movements.
> (John Holt)

To most of the people reading this book, this kind of hotheaded fanaticism is fairly easily dismissed in recalling the many little successes and worthwhile developments they have been able to help develop in their pupils. To most of us, Holt's call for children to have the right to direct and manage their own education reflects a naive romanticism which could do little to help pupils to overcome the realities of a harsh economic world. And yet, this is exactly the principle which is currently informing highly successful innovations in reporting procedures in many schools.

Regardless of the straitjacket of public examinations, there is evidence that many schools are beginning to develop reporting systems which relate explicitly to the needs of all pupils on leaving school. A recent survey in Scotland[5] showed that about one school in five issued its own school-leaving report and these varied considerably throughout the country.

Putting theory into practice

As we have suggested, school reporting systems are likely to seek to fulfil three needs. First and foremost, they are likely to be designed as part of the overall educational strategy of the school, helping to rein-force the pursuit of those learning outcomes — cognitive and non-cognitive— which teachers believe are worthwhile and necessary for youngsters leaving school at the present time. Second, such reports are likely to be designed to provide a good basis for communication with parents and with the pupils themselves so that they are a helpful source of guidance about course and career decisions. Third, the reports will be designed with the needs of employers and tertiary education in mind since particularly in an era of massive youth unemployment, no innovation in school reports can afford not to put the highest priority on helping youngsters to find a niche in the wider world. Despite the fact that most such initiatives are essentially 'grass-roots' developments born out of the spontaneous concern of individual teachers, they manifest a remarkable similarity of concern within a great variety of contexts. Certainly there has been some small measure of 'cross-fertilisation'. A more powerful force, however, has been an incontrovertible educational logic which has led those who have stopped to think about how to make comprehensive education more than just a form of school organisation to pursue similar goals in their reporting procedures. What these goals are is most readily made apparent in looking at a number of these spontaneous developments in reporting, and to this we now turn.

1 Evesham High School

Our first example is a former secondary technical school, 'a not untypical market-town comprehensive developing from a bilateral base',[6] whose catchment area includes both urban and rural communities. At Evesham, a number of staff were concerned over the demoralising and limiting effects of the traditional examination-based curriculum — particularly for low-achieving pupils. In what was, traditionally at least, an area of high employment, the teachers' principal concern was to offer a variety of educational goals so that all pupils could experience some degree of achievement whilst at school. At the same time, it was felt that the recognition of a much wider range of educational goals would be valuable in encouraging pupils to develop all sorts of personal qualities and interests in preparation for their future work or leisure, qualities which were largely ignored by traditional forms of reporting. As these ideas crystallised into explicit proposals other concerns were manifest: that the recording procedure developed should be useful to employers and thus help generally to bring school and industry closer together as well as specifically operating as an aid to career guidance and suitable job placement; that the procedure should be complementary to the more traditional work of the school, not placing too great a burden on staff or jeopardising pupils' prospects in

117

public examinations.

The first attempt to meet these needs took the form of a 'Leaving Certificate', an attempt which the school acknowledges to have been a disastrous failure. Like so many other unsuccessful attempts to innovate a worthwhile 'leaving certificate', this approach failed in not departing sufficiently from traditional approaches to reporting. It was stamped with classroom attitudes, teacher-dominated, not oriented to the needs of employers and, overall, highly negative in its effects.

So, Evesham High School went back to the drawing board and produced the 'Personal Achievement Record' which has proved so far to be highly successful. Neither an examination nor a report, the PAR is open to all fifth-year pupils but not compulsory; it involves almost no extra work and does not affect normal school work except in the improvement to self-knowledge and self-esteem which the provision of a reliable and valid record of specific achievements can bring.

The record consists of a plastic-covered, pocket-sized logbook which is issued to fifth-year pupils who ask their form tutor for it, together with a brief instruction pack about its completion. Parents too are sent a letter explaining the procedure and inviting their support. In the first full year of the scheme's operation, 200 out of 260 fifth-year pupils participated, those opting out being pupils not concerned with job prospects — the very high achievers or those pupils already fixed up with some kind of employment. In its second year of operation participation rose to 250 out of 270 fifth-year pupils.

The logbook has three sections.

(1) The first section, which is shown in Figure 6.1, allows for the pupil to enter for school authentication, details of the courses he is following, of any attainment tests associated with those course and mock and final examination results.

(2) The main part of the record is a printed list of 60 specific skills (Figure 6.2), chosen after long discussions between employers and school staff. The skills are divided into four equal groups — language, mathematics, practical skills and personal and social skills. The skills are more or less specific — but both specific skills, such as 'can swim 25m.' or 'can use a sewing machine' and more general attainments such as 'can work well as a member of a group', involve quite explicit criteria of mastery agreed on by the staff involved. Thus 'is able to use a calculator' involves a test administered by a member of the maths staff and opportunity is presented at regular intervals for the pupil to take or re-take this particular test. If the teacher is satisfied that the skill is genuinely mastered, she stamps the appropriate space in the logbook and signs it. If the pupil has not mastered the skill concerned, the teacher will explain what still remains to be done and the pupil can

re-take the test later. The form teacher keeps a master record — essential in cases of lost records, but valuable too for counselling purposes.

EVESHAM HIGH SCHOOL PERSONAL ACHIEVEMENT RECORD	Course followed		
	The following subjects have been studied during the last two years at the levels shown		
	Subjects	level	trial exam result
Name of student: _____ date of birth: _____ date of leaving: _____			
	Date: Form Tutor:		

Figure 6.1

(3) The third 'personal achievements' section allows the pupil to enter details of his or her own interests including school teams, hobbies, social service or anything else the pupil feels is important to record. Once again, the entry is authenticated by a teacher. The PAR is completed by Easter of the fifth year and is then signed by the head and the chairman of the governors.

Much of the scheme's success up to now is a direct result of the involvement of an enthusiastic group of local employers who as a result of advertisements and articles in the local press, became involved in the scheme through its compilation stages and subsequently donated the initial funding for materials. Equally important is the fact that local employers have agreed to ask for the logbook whenever a pupil from the school is interviewed. This scheme has now been running for two years and it is too early to predict its long-term value once the novelty has worn off. At present, pupils are guardedly keen, but their enthusiasm varies with their morale as a whole. Certainly teachers have found the exercise of producing specific lists of skills highly beneficial to their

LANGUAGE SKILLS

		STAFF	STAMP
1.	Has legible handwriting		
2.	Can write simple sentences		
3.	Can read and understand a popular newspaper		
4.	Can use simple punctuation correctly		
5.	Avoids elementary spelling mistakes		
6.	Can write a personal letter		
7.	Can give and take a telephone message		
8.	Can accurately complete a passport application		
9.	Regularly borrows from school or public library		
10.	Can write a business letter		
11.	Can make an accurate written report		
12.	Can make a clear spoken report		
13.	Can summarise accurately a notice or report		
14.	Can understand simple instructions in a foreign language		
15.	Can give simple instructions in a foreign language		

MATHS SKILLS

		STAFF	STAMP
1.	Has a good understanding of the rules of number		
2.	Has a good accuracy in handling numbers		
3.	Can apply the four rules to money with accuracy		
4.	Capable of performing everyday calculations in money with accuracy		
5.	Understands money transactions such as wages and income tax		
6.	Able to handle decimals met in everyday life		
7.	Able to handle fractions met in everyday life		
8.	Understand simple percentages		
9.	Understands simple profit and loss		
10.	Understands metric system of measure		
11.	Understands English measures of length, weight & capacity		
12.	Can measure accurately		
13.	Is able to use a calculator		
14.	Has an understanding of V.A.T.		
15.	Can read and understand time tables, wage tables and ready reckoner		

Figure 6.2   The Evesham P.A.R.

teaching and the specific, more short-term objectives thereby produced, more motivating for the majority of pupils for whom the 'deferred gratification' of the long-term, often unrealistic, targets of conventional academic courses offered little incentive. Initially, of course, teachers were concerned about the extra work involved, and about the difficulties in mastery, rather than graded, assessment, since criteria cannot be totally unambiguous. Some parents were concerned about possible 'certificates of failure' where a pupil did not appear to have many achievements. Inevitably there are practical problems such as interviews coming up before pupils have had a chance to be tested. None of these have proved to be a significant problem as yet and in the long term it is apathy in the face of the iron grip of public examinations which is likely to prove the strongest foe. Whatever happens in the long run, teachers at Evesham do feel that they have found an important alternative basis to traditional forms of school record in which an almost exclusive concern with academic achievement and inter-pupil comparison which served only to lower motivation in reinforcing failure has

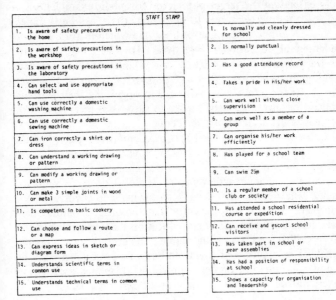

PRACTICAL SKILLS

	STAFF	STAMP
1. Is aware of safety precautions in the home		
2. Is aware of safety precautions in the workshop		
3. Is aware of safety precautions in the laboratory		
4. Can select and use appropriate hand tools		
5. Can use correctly a domestic washing machine		
6. Can use correctly a domestic sewing machine		
7. Can iron correctly a shirt or dress		
8. Can understand a working drawing or pattern		
9. Can modify a working drawing or pattern		
10. Can make 3 simple joints in wood or metal		
11. Is competent in basic cookery		
12. Can choose and follow a route or a map		
13. Can express ideas in sketch or diagram form		
14. Understands scientific terms in common use		
15. Understands technical terms in common use		

PERSONAL AND SOCIAL SKILLS

	STAFF	STAMP
1. Is normally and cleanly dressed for school		
2. Is normally punctual		
3. Has a good attendance record		
4. Takes a pride in his/her work		
5. Can work well without close supervision		
6. Can work well as a member of a group		
7. Can organise his/her work efficiently		
8. Has played for a school team		
9. Can swim 25m		
10. Is a regular member of a school club or society		
11. Has attended a school residential course or expedition		
12. Can receive and escort school visitors		
13. Has taken part in school or year assemblies		
14. Has had a position of responsibility at school		
15. Shows a capacity for organisation and leadership		

Figure 6.3   The Evesham P.A.R.

been replaced by three important new principles — close collaboration with the host community, particularly employers; emphasis on mastery rather than grading, and pupil-initiated, rather than teacher-initiated assessment.

We have chosen this case study to illustrate the scope for initiative by an individual school in instituting new forms of reporting which match the school's educational aims. Other initiatives of this kind in other schools typically share the concern at Evesham for a record which seeks to make education relevant for *all* pupils in the school by providing for the recognition of a wide range of important skills and interests.[7] Two of the most well-known of such schemes are the Scottish 'Pupil Profile' system and the Swindon Record of Personal Achievement (RPA). Both schemes have been covered extensively in existing publications[8] and so will be only briefly described here. Indeed, the extent of press coverage given to these schemes in itself reflects the novelty of the proposals and the widespread awareness that reform within the existing structure of public examinations cannot, by itself, account for the diverse ambitions and talents of all pupils passing through the educational system. Teachers have known for a long time that simply extending the target population for public examinations or inventing new ones merely serves to perpetuate the enormously expensive and time-consuming examination machine which in turn prevents any broadening of educational objectives. Many have felt frustrated that even the freedom of Mode III courses is constrained by the need to rank and grade pupils according to 'approved' syllabuses. There has been little scope for pupils' own initiative in organising their learning, little emphasis on any diagnostic aspect to such assessment, and little freedom to depart from traditional academic pursuits.

In 1976, however, the Manpower Services Commission published the results of a survey which showed clearly how much more emphasis employers of school-leavers put on personal characteristics and skills than on formal academic achievement. These figures are simply a reflection of what employers have been saying consistently over a number of years[9] but it is only recently that the bleak unemployment figures have served at last to convince educationists in general that new forms of recording and reporting pupils' achievement are urgently needed. Official recognition of this need has now been vouchsafed by the DES and co-ordination of development work in this area is now being actively pursued by research teams at the Schools Council.

TABLE 6.1

| | Considered essential for | | | |
	All grades of work %	Skilled manual work %	Unskilled manual work %	Non-manual work %
Willingness/attitude to work	76	80	81	70
Basic 3Rs	50	52	21	67
Good levels of numeracy	39	40	13	55
Good written English Literate	36	21	6	67
Specific Educational Qualifications	23	21	2	38

(Taken from 'Young People and Work', Manpower Studies No. 1, 1978, Manpower Services Commission, London, HMSO, Table 1, chapter 7.)

2 Pupils in profile

In Scotland, however, the need for a recording scheme which would meet the needs of all pupils for self-knowledge, for curricular and vocational guidance, and for a relevant and useful leaving report was recognised by the Headteachers' Association as early as 1972. A working party was set up which included representatives of industry, higher education, HMI, education authorities as well as head teachers and researchers. Their goal was to design an assessment procedure which would be able to offer all pupils recognition of their various talents through the assessment of many qualities not included in traditional reports. Further, such assessments were not to distinguish between more and less important activities or different categories of pupils (certificate/non-certificate). Community service or hill walking were to rank equally with science or history in the opportunity they afforded for the pupil to demonstrate his positive qualities. It was assumed that the precise operation of such a scheme would vary from school to school and hence would depend on a variety of different assessment techniques and recording schemes which would nevertheless have in common the effort to make as little demand as possible on teachers' time. It was decided, too, that although the final 'school-leaving report' must be amenable to external validation and moderation if it was to have more than a local currency, the recording and reporting procedure which fed into it should be such that it could provide for feedback and guidance to teachers, parents and pupils at every stage of a child's school career.

In the five years of research and development work which followed, the Scottish initiative pioneered the idea of 'profile' assessment in which major aspects of learning – basic skills, subject studies and personal qualities – were further broken down into various relevant components. In this way teachers could contribute their knowledge of individual pupils in all its variety and those using the record – other teachers, parents, employers and indeed the pupils themselves – could equally be presented with the richness of idiosyncratic detail which characterises any individual and which is equally grossly disregarded whether the epithet is 'less able' or 'bright'.

Figure 6.4 shows the class assessment sheet on which individual teachers record the knowledge they have gained of the different attributes of pupils as they have had opportunity to observe them in the various activities of school life. Figures 6.5 and 6.6 show how these assessments are organized into a 'pupil profile'. The report is so designed that it is not only able to record the whole range of pupil achievements but is also designed so that as far as possible it is a positive record of

S.C.R.E PROFILE ASSESSMENT SYSTEM — CLASS ASSESSMENT SHEET	Pupil's Name	O'Quarry	T Johnson	F Fielding	S Roberts	E Drake	H Holmes	D Kennedy	G McGregor	R James	L Fraser	M Jackson	E Dunn	S Smith	D Gordon	K McIntosh	P Anderson	F Lee				
	Class Group	3L	3L	3L	3L	3L	3L	3L	3L	3L	3L	3L	3L	3L	3L	3L	3L				
Skills	Listening	2	3	2	4	2	1	3	1	2	2	4	2	3	1	3	3	4	2		
	Speaking	2	4	1	3	3	2	3	2	2	4	4	1	1	3	3	1	4	2		
	Reading	1	2	2	3	2	1	2	2	3	2	3	2	5	2	3	4	3	1		
	Writing	2	3	1	4	3	1	3	2	4	2	4	2	4	3	4	4	2			
	Visual understanding & expression	4	3	1	3	4	3	2			1	3	3	3		2	3		2		
	Use of Number																				
	Physical Coordination																				
	Manual Dexterity			4		2	1				4			3				1			
Performance	Knowledge	1	4	3	4	3	1	4	2	3	4	3	3	4	1	3	4	4	1		
	Reasoning	2	3	2	3	2	1	3	1	1	2	4	3	3	2	4	4	4	1		
	Presentation	3	3	1	3	4	2	1	1	4	1	2	2	5	4	2	3	3	2		
	Imagination	2	4	1	1	3	2	2	1	1	3	4	2	1	3	3	3	4	3		
	Critical Awareness	2	3	2	2	4	1	3	2	1	2	4	2	2	2	4	4	4	2		
	Composite Grade	2	3	2	3	3	1	3	1	2	1	4	2	3	2	3	4	4	2		
	Perseverance	1	3	2	4	4	1	6	2	4	4	1	3	4	1	3	3	1	1		
	Enterprise	3	4	1	1	3	1	3	2	1	3	3	2	1	3	3	2	4	3		
	Subject/Activity																				
	Teacher																				
	Date																				

Figure 6.4   Teacher Assessment Form
Note: The information on these class sheets is collated twice annually into a 'pupil profile' as Figure 6.5 shows, and ultimately provides the information for a school-leaving report (Figure 6.6).

achievement rather than a negative record of failure. The Evesham High School report has been strongly influenced by the Scottish scheme, notably in the way individual skills are broken down into detailed and specific mastery criteria and the division of the report into the three sections of course assessment, skills and personal achievement.

3 Personal records

There are, however, profound differences between the Evesham approach and the Scottish scheme, and while the latter is still something done by teachers to or for pupils, in the Evesham approach, the responsibility for the record is the pupil's alone. This inspiration comes from the scheme's other parent, the Swindon Record of Personal Achievement. Central to the thinking behind this scheme and the associated later developments in Devon — 'The Record of Personal

Experience, Qualities and Qualifications', and the 'Diamond Challenge Programme' – is that pupils' own statements about their activities, their interests, their achievements, written in their own handwriting and uncorrected, are highly rewarding and educational for the pupil, and, at the same time, provide a wealth of information for the potential employer.

The RPA was designed to be compiled over a period of two academic years. As well as recording items on individual cards kept in a binder, each pupil has a diary and after discussion with his tutor, the pupil transfers some of the diary entries in more depth to one of the twenty-nine different kinds of record card in his folder. The Record of Personal Experience, Qualities and Qualifications is even less structured in that it is in no sense a diary or a curriculum vitae. It is not a self-assessment. It is simply an astonishingly revealing record of those things which a pupil feels to be worthy of note about himself, things which public examinations cannot, by definition, record. Many pupils categorised as 'remedial' or 'lazy' at school reveal considerable talent and enthusiasm in out of school pursuits such as camping, training animals, or making models. Some engage in reliable and unglamorous social services like reading to blind people; others are revealed by their records to be coping with considerable problems at home.

In no sense is the record intended to replace traditional forms of assessment. Rather it is intended to encourage the development of personal qualities by providing for the overt recognition of the richness and uniqueness of individual experience. At first glance, a typical entry may seem mundane.[10]

Making up a Bicycle

I made up a bicycle for myself. I got the frame off a friend of mine.
Then I painted it red and white. I bought a pair of handle bars,
back wheel and two tyres. I found the seat, the stem and the front
wheel in a dump. I then put all that on and I had some brakes and
fitted them on and made sure they work all right. Then I put a
dynamo on and put some new bulbs in the lights.

In fact, this entry, authenticated by the boy's father, reveals a good deal of determination and initiative, as well as interest and skill and is typical of the simple yet revealing entries such records provide.

It is often very difficult for teachers to make the initial adjustment required in supervising the preparation of this kind of record. Not only must they show genuine interest, but they must be willing to accept the pupil in terms of his own values and aspirations. It must be the pupil who decides what is to go into the record and what are the values

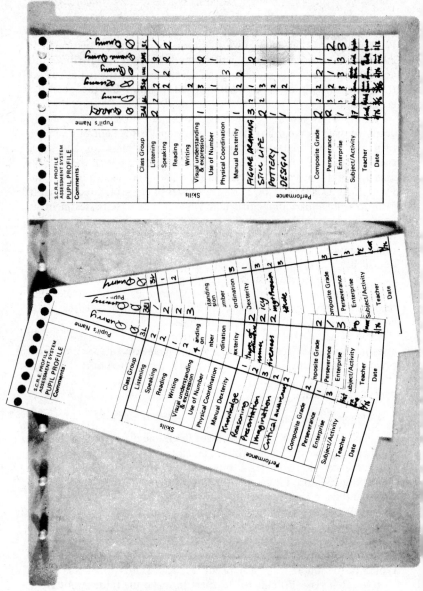

Figure 6.5   Manual mounting on a peg-board of assessment records relating to a single pupil. Records awaiting are shown to the left. Each slip comes from a different teacher and is a duplicate of a single column of the teacher assessment sheet shown in Figure 6.4

OTHER OBSERVATIONS

(includes other school activities, other awards and comments on positive personal qualities)

Notes
The grades A – D represent approximately 25% of the year group in each case.

The skill gradings represent a consensus derived from the individual ratings of each teacher's knowledge and reflect the standard obtained by the pupil with reasonable consistency.

All the information contained in this report is based on profile assessments,contributed by each teacher on a continuous and cumulative basis, including observations of personal qualities and informal activities.

SCHOOL LEAVING REPORT

This is a brief report on _____ Date of Birth _____

who completed class _____ School _____

in _____

and left on _____

This report is the result of continuous assessment by all the teachers of this pupil and has the authority of :–

Head Teacher _____

Director _____

SKILLS

LISTENING
Acts independently and intelligently on complex verbal instructions ☐

Can interpret and act on most complex instructions ☐

Can interpret and act on straightforward instructions ☐

Can carry out simple instructions with supervision ☐

READING
Understands all appropriate written material ☐

Understands the content and implications of most writing if simply expressed ☐

Understands uncomplicated ideas expressed in simple language ☐

Can read most everyday information such as notices or simple instructions ☐

VISUAL UNDERSTANDING AND EXPRESSION
Can communicate complex visual concepts readily and appropriately ☐

Can give a clear explanation by sketches and diagrams ☐

Can interpret a variety of visual displays such as graphs or train timetables ☐

Can interpret single visual displays such as roadsigns or outline maps ☐

PHYSICAL CO-ORDINATION
A natural flair for complex tasks ☐

Mastery of a wide variety of movements ☐

Can perform satisfactorily most everyday movements ☐

Can perform single physical skills such as lifting or climbing ☐

SPEAKING
Can debate a point of view ☐

Can make a clear and accurate oral report ☐

Can describe events orally ☐

Can communicate adequately at conversation level ☐

WRITING
Can argue a point of view in writing ☐

Can write a clear and accurate report ☐

Can write a simple account or letter ☐

Can write simple messages and instructions ☐

USE OF NUMBER
Quick and accurate in complicated or unfamiliar calculations ☐

Can do familiar or straightforward calculations, more slowly if complex ☐

Can handle routine calculations with practice ☐

Can do simple whole number calculations such as giving change ☐

MANUAL DEXTERITY
Has fine control of complex tools and equipment ☐

Satisfactory use of most tools and equipment ☐

Can achieve simple tasks such as wiring a plug ☐

Can use simple tools, instruments and machines such as a screwdriver or type writer ☐

SUBJECT/ACTIVITY ASSESSMENT

Curriculum Area	Subjects Studied (includes final year level where relevant)	Years of Study	Achievement	Enterprise (includes flair creativity)	Perseverance (includes reliability carefulness)
Aesthetic Subjects					
Business Studies					
Community/Leisure Activities					
Crafts					
English					
Mathematics					
Other Languages					
Outdoor Studies					
Physical Education					
Science					
Social Subjects					

Figure 6.6   School Leaving Record. The entries on this record are derived from the series of profile records cumulated during the years preceding leaving

127

and priorities it will reflect without any interference or 'vetting' or attempts to improve it from the teacher.

The Swindon RPA was the subject of a recent Schools Council evaluation[11] which revealed that in the 70 schools in which it is in use, it tends not surprisingly to be confined to the 'less able' pupils and that partly in consequence, employers as yet set little store by it. The cost of such a procedure which requires funding to be found for relatively expensive materials over and above that already spent on examinations may prove to be a significant stumbling block in the current economic climate. Teachers, however, remain convinced of its value in motivating pupils and in developing their personal qualities and self-respect. As use of the RPE grows slowly in Devon and in Nottinghamshire, a third scheme, 'The Diamond Challenge Programme', has recently been introduced, a procedure which is particularly suitable for the less structured settings of further education. In this programme, youngsters must undertake six activities which they plan in consultation with a tutor. As they evaluate their successes and failures it is hoped that they will learn to take more responsibility for themselves, to learn about themselves and to recognise that they can make things happen. It is for the students themselves to say: 'I am like this . . . . This is what I can do . . . . This is where I am going.'

The philosophy behind these various 'records' is expressed as follows by their creator, Don Stansbury:[12]

> The main purpose of recording is educational. It helps youngsters to know themselves and to take more control of their lives and their futures. It also may help the school by providing the basis of a better relationship based on respect for all kinds of gifts and abilities. If it also helps some youngsters to get jobs and some employers to know with more certainty, the character and style of applicants then that is a bonus. It could have an economic effect by encouraging enterprise and self-reliance. If, as seems certain, unemployment remains then recording is just as essential for those who cannot hope for jobs because they also need something on which to build some self-respect and to know what their own resources are.

These examples illustrate clearly a theme which runs consistently through the various attempts that are being made in schools throughout the country to institute more relevant forms of reporting. This theme is the way in which the diverse functions of reporting are given emphasis within any one system. We may identify these diverse functions in general terms as:

1 educational: allowing pupils to be in charge of their own recording and reporting in order to develop their self-knowledge and self-esteem and to encourage them to take responsibility for their own learning (allowing pupils to be in charge of their own learning is a further extension of this approach);
2 communication: providing a fairly standard basis for communication between parents, teachers and pupils.
3 diagnosis: providing a detailed, cumulative record of a pupil's progress so that suitable encouragement and help can be given as appropriate;
4 selection: providing a sound and convincing basis for the communication of relevant information to potential employers.

It is readily apparent that the Scottish pupil profile system puts more emphasis on functions 2-4, whereas the Evesham PAR and the RPA and RPE put particular weight on 1 and 4. The emphasis individual schools choose to place on each of these aspects will vary with local conditions and needs, but it is readily apparent that, whatever the balance between these different functions, a coherent school recording and reporting system will give some attention to all four. As such, its real and potential utility more than justifies the time spent on it. Its typically lowly place in comparison to public and even school examinations is correspondingly brought into question since the scope of such assessments is so much more limited.

Indeed, novel as such attempts to design a coherent assessment policy are, there are many who believe that any scheme which seeks merely to supplement the assessments made by external examinations or to be independent of them, is doomed to failure. They believe that initiatives which seek to extend public reporting to all pupils, which incorporate a measure of pupil involvement, which are the product of collaboration between teacher, pupil and parent, or which are concerned to include a much greater range of qualities, are all equally doomed to have little impact on the experience of schooling which for many pupils is at best irrelevant. It is this substantial body of opinion that believes only the abolition of traditional forms of public examination will allow schools to pursue the educational values reflected in such novel reporting schemes. This is partly because the scope for new approaches to teaching and curriculum organisation is so severely curtailed by the constraints of external examination syllabuses. That this is so is evidenced by the more and more traditional nature of classroom activity as a pupil progresses upward through the education system from the infants class towards the public examination stage.

In their recent book,[13] Burgess and Adams provide us with what is perhaps the most coherent set of proposals for supplanting examinations

129

and integrating curriculum and assessment in a way which genuinely seeks to recognise the radical changes in the process of schooling which have already taken place; a recognition made yet more urgently necessary by imminent, large-scale social and economic revolutions. In the Burgess and Adams scheme, the pupil would be required to draw up a personal 'itinerary' with his tutor at age fourteen for an individual programme of work over the next two years. This programme would be subject to constant monitoring by pupil and tutor collaboratively and would culminate in a statement that would be a positive account of the student's attributes, competencies and interests. Although successfully pioneered in higher education,[14] this scheme has yet to be tried in a school and indeed it will be a courageous head teacher who decides to lead his staff through such major (but not impracticable) changes in timetable organisation, in working relationships with pupils and colleagues; in relations with interested parties outside the school, and with external validating bodies. Most will be tempted to wait for a clearer lead. They can choose not to wait for such a lead, however. So much is clear from the experience of a determined group of teachers in Victoria, South Australia who provide our final, and most radical case study.

4 The Victoria experience

Once again the stimulus to this experiment — this time in '18+' reporting — was the widespread dissatisfaction among both teachers and some higher education institutions with the existing 'Higher School Certificate'. This examination was felt to place an undesirable constraint on schools and in particular to discriminate against certain class and ethnic groups. The group of schools who came together in support of an alternative proposal — 'The Secondary Tertiary Certificate' were committed to an approach very similar to those described above, namely student involvement in both individual curriculum planning and assessment, and an entirely non-competitive descriptive approach to assessment.[15] Standards between schools are kept roughly comparable by the work of six inter-school consultative committees — English, social science, maths, science, commerce, and arts, which agree on expectations and requirements. In this way the scheme overcomes the shortcomings of many such initiatives in the past, namely their lack of comparability. Although in every case the award of the STC depends on the successful completion of twelve units of study, schools are free to decide the content of courses in consultation with the students concerned. Every effort is made to include an element of work-experience in the study. The aim is to reach a realistic assessment of a student's aims and capabilities, an aim which requires a careful collaborative statement of objectives at the outset of the course. The outcome is an STC certificate which states the number of successful units completed; detailed written academic reports of the work done in each subject, a tertiary recommendation report where relevant and a student's personal evaluation of his aims, his abilities and his experience. Thus in one school, specific goals are decided upon for each subject twice a term by teachers and pupils. At the end of this period, oral and written evaluation takes place of progress made. These goals are likely to include not only academic objectives but participation in the life of the school as a whole.

It remains to be seen what the fate of STC will be, particularly in view of the new Victorian Institute of Secondary Education's attempt to incorporate it in a revised Higher School Certificate. Whatever happens, it is already clear that with the sympathetic co-operation of parents, pupils, employers, teacher unions and at least some institutes of higher education, teachers can make a significant attempt to break the stranglehold of public examinations without waiting for such reforms to be nationally instituted.

Conclusion

It is fitting that this should be the last major chapter in this book. Partly this is because the most crucial issues in reporting arise at the end of schooling and partly because questions pertaining to terminal reporting — what, when, to whom, how — encapsulate all the various questions of why, what and how to record raised in the earlier chapters in this book. The thinking behind the various reporting schemes described in this chapter is ultimately applicable to six- or sixteen-year-olds. What goes into a report will reflect a school's approach to diagnostic assessment, to evaluating achievement, to non-cognitive assessment, for this is the school's formal presentation of its work or a reflection of its ethos. The way in which a school generates and records information about its pupils is significant in determining the information that will be available to inform teaching. But it is much more significant in focusing the attention of teachers and students in particular ways.[16] It is for this reason that we have dwelt to a considerable extent in this chapter on the not immediately relevant issue of public examinations. Ultimately, it is procedures at this point which determine, to a greater or a lesser extent, educational priorities and the constraints within which teachers can pursue their own objectives. It is vital that we ask

131

ourselves whether the kinds of information we collect and send out about pupils truly reflect our educational aims. Frequently an examination of curriculum and assessment practice will reveal a disjuncture between the two. When two forces are operating in opposite directions, the effect is frequently nil.

Chapter 7

Old Normgrade revisited

In this book we have looked at a variety of different ways in which assessment procedures can help the individual teacher keep track of an individual pupil's progress and responses. We have shown how variable the particular procedures used must be if they are to reflect and be useful in the wide variety of teaching and learning situations now found in both primary and secondary schools. Clearly, 'keeping track of teaching' takes place at a number of levels and, as we saw in chapter 5, a way must be found of co-ordinating the diverse insights of the classroom teacher to provide for comparison of a pupil's progress in different subjects, to provide the basis for subject choice and curriculum guidance and even to provide some indication of the performance of the school itself.

In the last chapter we extended our concern beyond the integration of assessment with classroom teaching to include a consideration of ways of communicating information about pupils for parents, potential employers and for tertiary education.

To introduce these discussions we offered a case study of a mythical school – Old Normgrade Grammar – in which the co-existence of traditional and innovative ideas was giving rise to a variety of policy disagreement between departments. Assessment was seen to be one of the main bones of contention. It is fitting that in the last chapter we should look at some of the difficulties schools have encountered in coming to terms with the new demands being made upon them by the sorts of change in educational philosophy and organisation which have overtaken nearly all schools in one way or another in recent years.

Towards a school assessment policy

One of the biggest problems at Old Normgrade was the differing assessment priorities of different departments, highlighting the need for some co-ordination of assessment policy and practice at school level. The formulation of such a policy capable of embracing the very different personalities, teaching styles and curriculum content inevitably involved is perhaps the most difficult stage in the evolution of new styles of 'keeping track of teaching'. It has thus been left to the final chapter of this book to give greater consideration to the formulation of a coherent school assessment policy, a position which has no bearing on its importance, since without this co-ordination, major stumbling blocks to the approaches to assessment advocated in this book are likely to occur.

As we will argue below, a coherent, receptive and dynamic school assessment policy, while not essential to the development of individual initiatives from teachers or groups of teachers, is far more likely to nurture useful innovation than implicit, haphazard assumptions that, as the system has 'worked' for the last fifteen years, then it is best to let sleeping dogs lie. Amongst the points we would make to substantiate this assertion are, first, that where there is an unsupportive school policy, far from being encouraged to develop new forms of classroom assessment, those teachers who do try, are likely to come in for a degree of criticism and, at best, as we have seen in many of the preceding case studies, a requirement for the kind of information their assessment techniques are not designed to provide. Second, where there is no logical relationship between classroom, department and school assessment, recording and reporting, not only is a lot of valuable information likely to be lost 'in the system', but the school itself will not be communicating a coherent ethos to its pupils. In certain cases the school may find itself without the kind of information it needs or the necessary machinery to ensure comparability between the various departments in their assessments.

Uphill in turmoil

Thus the provision of a coherent *school* assessment policy is logically an integral component of the process of instituting assessments which directly relate to curricular needs. Our last case study, whilst clearly fictional, is nevertheless modelled closely on the experiences of one, very typical, school, a school facing just such a concern, a school in which major upheavals in organisation and consequent curriculum dilemmas presented the most urgent need for an assessment policy to be found which could help the staff in the novel teaching situations in which they found themselves and, at the same time, allay concern on the part of parents and the education authority. The search for such a policy at Uphill clearly illustrates what we have identified as one of the biggest stumbling blocks in the co-ordination of individual classroom assessments, namely that teachers and departments can be as different in their assessment priorities as their pedagogic styles and curricular aims. The problem of providing for comparability between teachers and departments without imposing such constraints on individual teachers that assessment is no longer an integral part of teaching is nowhere better portrayed than in Uphill School.

Unlike Old Normgrade, where the only challenge to tradition came from the teachers themselves, Uphill was subject to all the upheaval reorganisation and a change in catchment area can provide. The school began as a four-form comprehensive 'creamed' by a grammar school and 'sedimented' by a secondary modern school. For some years it had been very traditional in its assessment policy — work was marked out of ten, classes were streamed, reports were entered in one line spaces on the traditional style form and everyone had formal examinations. Like many other schools, when the time came for it to be amalgamated with a nearby four-form-entry secondary modern school, Uphill was essentially unprepared and, apart from some attempt at syllabus co-ordination, retained its traditional organisation, the newcomers inhabiting the lower streams. With little enthusiasm, expertise or in-service training, the results were predictable.

With regard to assessment, departmental policy diverged widely at that time. The English department, convinced that mixed ability teaching gives a chance to 'stretch' every pupil, avoided giving a numerical mark. The head of English, Mrs Galahad, said they could not report adequately on a pupil in only one line. Miss Litmus, head of lower school science and Mr Punctilio, head of maths, stuck to the traditional four out of ten. Other teachers had more prosaic concerns. They complained that a class teacher had to go to four separate house staffrooms and queue for two separate boxes in each room to write the reports of one class. A new head teacher came. He sought to solve this problem by instituting a system of self-carbonating individual report slips. He suggested reports should be 'positive in approach'. It was unfortunate that Miss Earnest took positive approach to mean that you only said nice things about your pupils. However, with the firm conviction that more means better, the staff wrote longer reports and were well satisfied.

The next step against polarising ability groups too clearly was to abolish formal examinations below the fourth year in favour of class tests. This seemed to work well, apart from the continuing dissension between the 'comment only' and the two out of ten brigades, until the catchment area changed to provide a balanced, instead of a 'bottom-heavy' intake. The new parents' anxiety about public examination results was soon caught by the staff. The senior staff decided that the vertical house system with no agreed criteria for comparison between individual house heads worked against the setting and monitoring of standards. The school was reorganised horizontally for across the year monitoring and twice-annual assessment on a five-point scale was instituted for all pupils for attainment, effort and conduct. 'But how do I assess conduct?' asked Miss Beaver, the painstaking head of history. 'Flossie and Freda, in the fourth year, slumber at the back of my class pen in hand. When I walk round, they rouse themselves to write a line. They never do anything wrong because they never do anything. Should I give them a B or a C? Samantha, in the first year, is seldom still except when she is reading. She is interested in everything, has ideas about everything, frequently interrupts and writes illegible reams of imaginative historical fantasy. Do I give her D or E? Louise in the second year reads and writes conscientiously, never raising her head and never joining in. Her homework is uninspired but immaculate. Do I give her an A and send her to Child Guidance?' No answer was forthcoming.

Another problem was that despite the institution of objective cognitive ability tests in years 1 and 3, the Director of Education was becoming increasingly worried at the waste of time and effort involved in the many unclassified 'O' level results. It was decided that there must be standardised testing in the third year with an emphasis on identifying skills. This still left the problem of the English department's opposition to numerical testing and the history department, who wanted to know how they could design a standardised test for a course that was based largely on discussion and investigation. Nobody could tell them.

As the employment situation worsened, pressure from parents that their children be allowed to sit for 'O' levels increased. Third year parents' meetings for option choices were full of painful scenes. 'What is my professional position?' said Mr Punctilio, head of mathematics. 'How can a parent tell me his child is going to do 'O' level when I know she can't as her assessment is below average?'

Mr and Mrs Green were two parents who disputed Mr Punctilio's decision. Amanda wanted five 'O' levels for teacher training and mathematics had to be one. Amanda was recommended for the top CSE set since she came well below the 'O' level/CSE line. The head teacher supported Mr Punctilio's decision. Mr and Mrs Green wrote to their Member of Parliament. He wrote to the Director of Education who professed himself willing to support the school's decision provided there was proper evidence. The evidence was that Amanda's twice-annual assessments for the first two years had been 'A' in nearly all subjects including maths. The across-the-board test for third year maths had been marked by individual teachers and the marks unstandardised. Amanda happened to be taught by Mrs Hatchett, a good careful teacher who was making sure no mistake went unchecked. It was unfortunate that Mr Punctilio hadn't realised that mathematics marking can vary considerably from teacher to teacher both in terms of the degree of severity and in the spread of marks for the whole group. It was unfortunate that he hadn't standardised the marks of Amanda's class in relation to the rest ... Amanda was duly entered for the 'O' level course.

Her suspicions aroused, the head of lower school studied the second year assessments against the objective cognitive ability test results and proceeded to plot the curve. She was able to show the staff that in religious education, all the second year geese were swans, and that in geography, absolutely everyone was average. The staff were horrified at their continuing failure to establish a satisfactory assessment programme and asked for a 'teach-in'.

A school assessment policy emerges

Groups of staff met for a day at a time to consider the whole range of assessment problems. They considered what kind of information should go to parents, and how it could be made maximally informative and, at the same time, accurate. They considered forms of assessment other than the traditional written test and how discrepancies between teachers' judgments could be avoided. They considered how to reconcile the gulf between the approach to assessment emphasising motivation, dialogue and individual progress championed by the English department and that of the maths department, emphasising comparison and objectivity. They also went beyond existing problems and studied some other approaches to assessment they hadn't previously thought of − self-assessment, non-cognitive assessment − profiles − criterion-referenced tests.

Each department evolved its own solution. Some emphasised continuity and the importance of devising a check list of skills against which progress could be charted from year to year. Some sought to tackle the problem of maintaining the interest and motivation of the low-achieving pupil, whilst nevertheless avoiding a misleading report. Some considered the need to integrate assessment within, rather than at

English and Humanities in the First Year

FORM	completed during 1st term					completed during 2nd term			completed by the end of the year								COMMENTS
Names	Use of Atlas	Diagram/Map Drawing	Drawing/Use of Graphs	Use of O.S. maps	Detail of researched work	Understanding shown	Organisation of written material	Spelling	Reading	Sentences/ Punctuation	Oral Fluency	Imaginative Writing	Attitude to Work	Presentation			

Figure 7.1
Note: This sheet is completed on an A-E grading scale as it is passed between English, history and geography departments.

the end of curriculum units and whether an A-E grading was appropriate in this respect. They began to see the potential of assessment for providing evaluation of particular aspects of the curriculum. Indeed, a good deal of 'cross-fertilisation' took place between departments in which good ideas about assessment and curriculum were the currency.

The more they thought about what they were doing, the more the teachers at Uphill were appalled at some of their past practices. Equally, they were now well aware of the difficulty of reconciling clerical simplicity with informativeness and both of these with comparability. The various departmental report sheets, examples of which are reproduced here, show both the common themes in recording which resulted from these assessment discussions and the differing emphases which continued to characterise different departments.

In the second year the English department has its own written profile assessment under the following headings:

Reading
stories and poems
non fiction and reference books
Talking together
Drama
Writing
approaches and ways of working
products
Reading aloud
– in whole class playreading
– in small group playreading
– to whole class prepared reading
– on tape
– to teacher
– to group

There is also provision for pupil self-assessment in the form of a sheet on which the pupil can list the pieces of writing she wishes the teacher to note and comment upon, and another on which she can list her reading. The logical development of this kind of assessment is the completely open-ended 'essay' that teacher and pupil write about the pupil's progress in the subject higher up the school.

The third-year modern languages 'profile' shows a similar approach with graded assessments for 'oral ability' 'general conversation' 'aural comprehension' in both French and English, and written comment on 'written work' 'free composition' 'attitude' and 'parental contact' – a profile which gets progressively more detailed as the pupil progresses in the subject and his skills increase.

The science department have chosen a 'matrix' profile as shown in

139

First Year _____

Form _____

General Comment

Form Tutor _____

Science Tutor _____

Topics	Skills			Presentation	Attainment (test only) % grade	Conduct	Effort
	Practical	Observation	Interpretation				
Classification							
Water I							
Water II							
Measurement							
Reproduction							
Annual Assessment							

(A-E grading)

Figure 7.2

140

Figure 7.2 and have also provided detailed guidance for individual teachers as to the meaning of each grade.

Like many other schools, Uphill School is more than conscious of the need to work out a coherent assessment policy. Its struggles and pressures, its constraints and successes are recorded here simply because they are typical and offer a comprehensive picture of the interaction of the various assessment concerns with which we have been concerned in this book. Uphill is atypical, however, in its recognition of how far they still have to go in reconciling the conflicting assessment needs and effects. There is a large immigrant population at the school, many of them with language problems. Some way of relating assessment to the specific problems of this group has still to be found. Many of the pupils come from difficult backgrounds and lack both motivation and confidence — the teachers feel the development of self-assessment could help here. They want to develop the basis for a closer relationship with parents. It is this kind of problem which the school must now address.

Conclusions

We have written this book in the hope that other schools may be able to shortcut some of the agonies of Uphill by adapting practices which other schools have developed to suit their own assessment needs. Being wise after the event, can we identify how Uphill could have been helped in its dilemmas?

Perhaps the most important lesson Uphill needed to learn was to identify the purposes of different kinds of assessment — to distinguish between teaching-oriented diagnostic assessment and the rather different sort of assessment concerned with achievement — selection, reporting and accountability. In most schools there will be a Mrs Galahad and a Mr Punctilio with a whole range of opinion in between. Teachers who will differ in the emphasis they place on using assessment for motivation and who equally will differ in the kind of diagnostic feedback they wish to give their pupils. To some extent these differences are dictated by the nature of the subject — an emotive comment in maths would be as inappropriate as a 'right/wrong' decision in creative writing, but to some extent too such differences are the result of personality and the individual or departmental teaching style.

As far as diagnostic classroom assessment is concerned then, departments should have the freedom to devise their own procedures which reflect their curricular priorities. Diagnostic assessment, with all its advantages of motivation and relevance to the day-to-day needs of pupils should probably be the priority of a school assessment policy.

In turn such a policy throughout the school must eventually feed into a reporting system, but the tail must not be allowed to wag the dog. Indeed, a carefully thought out diagnostic assessment approach in each department which sets out clear criteria and defines the meaning of success in them will avoid the need to resort to statistical manipulation when inter-subject comparisons come to be made. We have seen examples of various ways in which this might be achieved in many of our case study schools and indeed at Uphill itself where the principle of profile assessment was common to a number of departments. A 'profile' is indeed an extremely useful approach to this problem, being sufficiently flexible to allow the recording of all kinds of information both cognitive and non-cognitive, either in words or grades. If carefully designed, such profiles can build up into a revealing and comprehensive record.

The other crucial lesson to be learned from the experiences of Uphill, as our study of Old Normgrade suggested, is the need for teachers to have as full as possible an understanding of the principles of assessment and in particular a clear notion of relating assessment techniques to specific criteria and not to broad generalisations. It would be Utopian and indeed undesirable to expect all teachers to become statistical experts in the manipulation of factor analyses, for example, but it is important that everyone charged with the responsibility of designing assessment systems should be aware of their reasons for making choices rather than accepting the word of 'experts', or even worse, doing only what they have done before. In this respect the schools have, in the form of the examination boards, a much more sophisticated model to question than does higher education where assessment techniques are still often quite amazingly naive.

Beyond this, our volume could not have offered Uphill any ready solution to its problem. It must be for the school itself and for individual teachers to decide whether self-assessment would be helpful, what emphasis to give non-cognitive assessment, how often to institute standardised tests, what proportion of diagnostic information to make available to parents, what form its leaving report should take . . . .

This book has set out to provide a framework for such discussions. It has set out to show the variety of techniques already pioneered in the classroom which individual teachers can adapt to meet their own needs. At the same time it has sought to relate the various levels of assessment concern within the school so that as well as embodying curricular aims, the assessment policy can reinforce the ethos and concerns of the school as a whole. The traumas associated with the evolution of such a policy are well illustrated by the experiences of Uphill School but, equally, so is the necessity for such a policy. In those schools which, unlike Old Normgrade Grammar, are seeking to respond positively to the new classroom demands brought about by mixed ability and individualised teaching, open-plan classrooms, ethnic diversity, social unrest and pressures for accountability, teachers are actively searching for more constructive and appropriate ways of 'keeping track of teaching'. This book has been written to help those already committed to that search.

Notes

1 The assessment scene

1 F.T. Wilhelms, 'Evaluation as Feedback' in R. Hooper (ed.), *The Curriculum: Context, Design and Development*, Edinburgh, Oliver & Boyd, 1971.

2 The Scottish Education Department Consultative Committee on the Curriculum, *The Structure of the Curriculum in the 3rd and 4th years of the Scottish Secondary School*, Edinburgh, HMSO, 1977. Recent public statements on the curriculum in England, such as the Department of Education and Science, *Framework for the Curriculum* (1980) and Her Majesty's Inspectorate, *Aspects of Secondary Education* (1980), are similar in tone.

3 K. Ingenkamp, *Educational Assessment*, Slough, NFER Publishing, 1977.

4 P.M. Broadfoot, *Assessment, Schools and Society*, London, Methuen, 1979.

5 A.C. Ryrie, A. Furst and M. Lauder, *Choices and Chances*, London, Hodder & Stoughton, 1979.

6 Scottish Council for Research in Education, *Pupils in Profile*, London, Hodder & Stoughton, 1977.

7 The education systems of the United Kingdom are almost unique internationally in their continued reliance on formal external examinations at the end of compulsory education (normally 16-plus).

8 J.P. Forsyth and W.B. Dockrell, *Curriculum and Assessment: the Response to Munn and Dunning*, Edinburgh, Scottish Council for Research in Education, 1979.

9 For example, legislation currently before Parliament will make a statutory obligation on local authorities to publish the external examination results on a school by school basis.

10 Many schools and local authorities are seeking to turn contemporary pressure for accountability into a positive force by attempting a

systematic review of the educational experiences offered to pupils in any one school. See, for example, Oxfordshire, ILEA, Solihull, etc.

11 H.D. Black and W.B. Dockrell, 'Assessment in the affective domain, Do we? Can we? Should we?', *British Educational Research Journal* vol. 6, no. 2, February 1980.

2 Problems in practice

1 See for example the SSRC 'Oracle' research of the University of Leicester School of Education especially in the recent volume *Progress and Performance in the Primary Classroom*, edited by M. Galton and B. Simon, London, Routledge & Kegan Paul, 1980.

2 This helpful distinction is made by Judah Schwartz, in the *Times Educational Supplement*, 16 November 1979, in an article entitled 'What is measurable?'

3 Keeping track of learning

1 Scottish Curriculum Development Service, Glasgow Centre, 'Mixed Ability Teaching in Geography: A Guidance Document' Occasional Paper, (A.Adam) Jordanhill College, Glasgow, 1979.

2 It is interesting that since the work took place in this department, school assessment policy has now changed and each subject has designed its own report form which relates to specific criteria which have been attained by the pupils.

3 G. Owens and L. Soule, 'The Individual Profile', *Forum*, vol. 13, Spring, 1971.

4 R. Glaser, 'Adapting the Elementary School Curriculum to Individual Performance' in R. Hooper (ed.), *The Curriculum: Context, Design and Development*, Edinburgh, Oliver & Boyd, 1971.

5 L.C. Taylor, *Resources for Learning*, Harmondsworth, Penguin, (2nd edn), 1972.

6 B.J. Bloom, *Human Characteristics and School Learning*, New York, McGraw Hill, 1976.

7 Tour de France, A Research and Development Project in Modern Languages directed by the National S1/S2 French Working Party of the Scottish Central Committee for Modern Languages and carried out at the University of Stirling under the direction of R. Johnston.

8 H.D. Black and W.B. Dockrell, *Diagnostic Assessment in Secondary Schools*, Edinburgh, Scottish Council for Research in Education, 1980. There are also specialised versions of this book for teachers of geography, technical education and home economics.

9 F.T. Wilhelms, 'Evaluation as Feedback' in Hooper, op. cit.

10 C. Ashby and P. Williams, 'A guide to children's assessment of

other children's topic writing'. Materials produced for 'Assessment in the Primary School' Course, University of Leicester School of Education, 1978.

11 P.M. Broadfoot, 'The affective role of assessment: a study of pupils' involvement in the assessment process', M.Ed. dissertation, University of Edinburgh, 1977. See also P.M. Broadfoot, 'Communication in the Classroom: a study of the role of assessment in motivation', *Educational Review*, vol. 31, no. 1, 1979.

12 These include such notions as 'Responsive Evaluation', 'Illuminative Evaluation', 'Democratic Evaluation', 'Programme Evaluation' and many others.

13 See, for example, P.M. Broadfoot op. cit. (both references) and R. Meighan, 'Consultation and Educational Ideologies: Some issues raised by research into children's judgments of teaching performance' in L. Barton and R. Meighan (eds), *Sociological Interpretations of Schooling in Classrooms*, Driffield, England, Nafferton, 1978.

14 N. Tucker, 'Asking the Customers', *Times Educational Supplement*, 29 February 1980.

15 Ibid.

16 See, for example, Meighan (1978) op. cit.

17 Exceptions to this generalisation include useful books such as: M. Shipman, *In School Evaluation*, London, Heinemann, 1979; W. Harlen (ed.), *Evaluation and the Teachers' Role*, London, Schools Council Research Studies, Macmillan, 1978.

4 'The ghost in the machine': keeping track of personal progress

1 B.S. Bloom, *Human Characteristics and School Learning*, New York, McGraw Hill, 1976.

2 V. Greany and T. Kellaghan, 'Cognitive and personality factors associated with the class placement of pupils', *Irish Journal of Education*, vol. 6, Winter edition, 1972.

3 R. Wood and I.W.A. Naphthali, 'Assessment in the Classroom', *Educational Studies*, vol. 1, number 3, 1975, pp. 151-61.

4 D. Ulich and W. Mertens (1973), 'Urteile über Schüler' (Weinheim, Beltz), quoted in K. Ingenkamp, *Educational Assessment*, Slough, NFER, 1977.

5 S. Brown and D. Macintyre, 'Differences among pupils in science classes: the contrast between teachers' perceptions and pupils' performance', St. Andrews, paper presented to Scottish Educational Research Association, annual conference, 1977.

6 A. Morrison, 'Formal and Informal Assessment in the Classroom', *Education in the North*, 1974, pp. 63-6.

7 R. Hoste and B. Bloomfield, 'Continuous Assessment in the CSE: Opinion and Practice', *Schools Council Examination Bulletin*, no.

31, London, Evans, 1975.

8   Scottish Council for Research in Education, *Pupils in Profile*, London, Hodder & Stoughton, 1977.

9   B. Doe, 'APU may drop personality testing', *Times Educational Supplement*, 15 February 1980.

10 See, for example, J. Raven, *Education, Values and Society*, London, H.K. Lewis, 1977.

11 Ingenkamp, op. cit.

12 In its most extreme form, the 'Revised Code' of the latter part of the nineteenth century instituted by Robert Lowe, teachers' salaries depended on their pupils demonstrating they had achieved the requisite standard not just in skills but in diligent application and morality.

13 W.B. Dockrell and J.P. Forsyth, *Curriculum and Assessment: the response to Munn and Dunning*, Edinburgh, Scottish Council for Research in Education, 1979.

14 H.D. Black and W.B. Dockrell, 'Assessment in the affective domain, Do we, Can we, Should we?' *British Educational Research Journal*, vol. 6, no. 2, February 1980. The mean correlation between the eight characteristics grouped as 'general class behaviour' was only 0.23.

15 C.D. Spielberger, *Anxiety and Behaviour*, New York, Academic Press, 1966.

15 K. Hope, 'Merit, Advantage and Deprivation in Scotland', unpublished manuscript, Oxford University, 1977.

17 V. Greany, 'Teachers' Perceptions of Pupils' Personality', *Irish Journal of Education*, vol. 8, 1974, pp. 89-101.

18 P.W. Airasian, T. Kellaghan and G.F. Madaus, 'The Stability of Teachers' Perceptions of Pupil Characteristics', *Irish Journal of Education*, vol. 11, pp. 74-84.

19 E. Kleiter, 'Über Referenz Interaktions und Korrelationsfehler im Lehrerurteil, Bildung und Erziehung', 26, pp. 100-17, quoted in Ingenkamp, op. cit.

20 Ingenkamp, op. cit.

21 W.J. Popham, *Educational Evaluation*, Englewood Cliffs, New Jersey, Prentice-Hall, 1975.

22 D.C. McClelland (1950) in G. Atkinson and D.C. McClelland, *Motives in Fantasy, Action and Society*, New York, Van Nostrand, 1958. See also Raven, op. cit., part XI.

23 Popham, op. cit.

24 H.D. Black and W.B. Dockrell, *Diagnostic Assessment in Secondary Schools*, Edinburgh, Scottish Council for Research in Education, 1980.

25 'Cut-off' Score is the term used to describe the score required to allow a pupil to be allocated to a 'mastery' category in criterion-referenced assessment. There is considerable literature on this, including substantial criticism of the 'arbitrary' nature of most

decisions. In this context, however, the arbitrary element is tempered by professional judgment and is thus an informed decision rather than a random decision.

26 S.A. Brown, 'Attitude Goals in Secondary School Science', *Stirling Educational Monographs*, No. 1, University of Stirling Department of Education, 1976.

5 Dealing with achievement: reporting, monitoring and the accountability issue

1 For further details, see J. Blanchard, 'English at Comberton Village College', in T. Burgess and E. Adams (eds), *Outcomes of Education*, London, Macmillan, 1980.

2 J. Blanchard, 'Getting into Profile', *Times Educational Supplement*, 29 February 1980.

3 See, for example, Scottish Council for Research in Education, *Pupils in Profile*, London, Hodder & Stoughton, 1977; and Edinburgh, Scottish Council for Research in Education National Survey on School Assessment and Reporting (unpublished).

4 A.C. Ryrie, A. Furst and M. Lauder, *Choices and Chances – a study of pupils' subject choices and future career intentions*, London, Hodder & Stoughton, 1979.

5 See, for example, E. Taylor, 'Damaging secrecy', *Times Educational Supplement*, 15 September 1978.

6 E. Davies, 'Primary School Records: St. Anne's First School', in Burgess and Adams, op. cit.

7 See National Foundation for Educational Research Newsletter, 1977, and The Schools Council record-keeping project, information from: Schools Council, Gt. Portland Street, London.

8 B. MacDonald, 'Accountability Standards and the Process of Schooling' in T. Becher and S. McLure (eds), *Accountability in Education*, Slough, NFER, 1978.

9 H. Simons, 'The Evaluative School', *Forum for the Discussion of New Trends in Education*, vol. 22, 1979.

10 MacDonald, op. cit.

11 G. Vernava, 'Self Assessment at a London Comprehensive', *Forum for the Discussion of New Trends in Education*, vol. 22, 1979.

12 ILEA, *Keeping the School Under Review*, London, Inner London Education Authority, 1977.

13 Simons, op. cit. The traditional HMI inspection provides a useful illustration of this argument.

14 MacDonald, op. cit.

15 Simons, op. cit.

16 G. Samuel, 'Think before you publish', *Times Educational Supplement*, 23 November 1979.

17 G.J. Pollock and W.G. Thorpe, *Standards of Numeracy in Central*

Region, Edinburgh, Scottish Council for Research in Education, 1979.

18 For example, B. Taylor, 'Somerset Home Grown Yardsticks', *Supplement to Education*, 21 September 1979.

19 National Foundation for Educational Research, Local Education Authorities and Schools' Item Banking Project, *General Brochure*, Slough, NFER, December 1978. (Project terminated in 1982).

20 For example, H. Goldstein, 'Consequences of using the Rasch Model for Educational Assessment', *British Educational Research Journal*, vol. 5, 1979, pp. 211-20.

21 It is interesting to note that it is the very fact that schools can vary so widely in their curriculum provision in Britain and other decentralised countries such as the United States that makes such monitoring necessary. In countries where curriculum and pedagogy are largely centrally prescribed (as, for example, in France) no such monitoring is typically regarded as necessary.

22 D. Nuttall, 'A Rash Attempt to Measure Changing Standards' in *Supplement to Education*, 21 September 1979.

23 Ibid.

24 W.B. Dockrell in 'Research in the Service of Education', the *Proceedings of the 50th Anniversary Conference*, Edinburgh, Scottish Council for Research in Education, 1978.

25 C. Selby, 'Assessing the APU', *Supplement to Education*, 21 September 1979.

26 See Dockrell, op. cit.

27 Quoted in W. Taylor, 'Values and Accountability' in Becher and McClure, op. cit.

28 For a discussion of the relationship, see P.M. Broadfoot, *Assessment, Schools and Society*, London, Methuen, 1979.

6 And so to work . . . the final reckoning

1 T. Burgess and E. Adams (eds), *Outcomes of Education*, London, Macmillan, 1980.

2 D. Stansbury, 'The Motivation and Documentation of School Leavers', *Final Progress Report of School-teacher Fellowship*, Exeter University, 1980.

3 M. Jackson, 'Half go from school to dole', *Times Educational Supplement*, 25 July 1980.

4 J. Holt, *Escape from Childhood*, Harmondsworth, Penguin, 1975.

5 Scottish Council for Research in Education, 'National Survey on School Assessment and Reporting', (unpublished), Edinburgh, 1980.

6 M. Duffy, 'A logbook of personal achievement', *Education*, 1 December 1980.

7 Many schools have taken up the Evesham High School model for

their own PAR such as the Market Weighton School, Humberside, or developed their own pupil leaving reports, such as Liberton High School, Edinburgh.

8   See Burgess and Adams, op. cit., for a concise description of both. Longer descriptions are available in *Pupils in Profile*, London, Hodder & Stoughton, 1977, and D. Stansbury, *RPE Tutor's Handbook*, RPE Publications, 25 Church Street, South Brent, Devon, 1976. The Schools Council have now published an evaluation of the RPA by T. Swales (1979).

9   See, for example, C. Townsend, 'School and Work' in Burgess and Adams, op. cit., and Scottish Council for Research in Education, *Pupils in Profile*, op. cit.

10 D. Stansbury, 'The Record of Personal Experience, Qualities and Qualifications', 1978 mimeo available from RPE publications.

11 Swales, op. cit.

12 D. Stansbury, 'The Motivation, Qualification and Employment of School Leavers', Report of a conference of teachers, 11-13 June 1979, South Hams Teachers Centre, Tresillian Kingsbridge, Devon.

13 Burgess and Adams, op. cit.

14 The example of North East London Polytechnic is now being taken up in a number of other centres. See J. Fairhall, *Education Guardian*, 2 December 1980.

15 P. Newell, 'Going the non-competitive way', *Times Educational Supplement*, 7 March 1980.

16 See, for example, M. Garet, 'Testing one, two, three', *Times Educational Supplement*, 16 November 1979, although the point is a familiar one to teachers.

Index

151